Theodore Olson

SPECIAL THANKS TO:

DORI'S BAKERY
IN TAOS, N.M.
FOR ENDLESS CUPS
OF COFFEE

AND TO MY
MOM
FOR LOVING SUPPORT
IN ALL MY STRANGE
UNDERTAKINGS

COVER ART: "TWIN FLAMES RISING"
COPYRIGHT 1991
BY SHEM EMMANUEL

COVER DESIGN AND CALLIGRAPHY: TERI MARTIN
11 LEONARD COURT
ALAMEDA, CA 94501
501-521-6075

SHINING LIGHT PRODUCTIONS
707 CONTINENTAL CIRCLE # 239
MT. VIEW, CA 94040
415-966-8387

THIS BOOK IS DEDICATED TO:

AREANA DRU

SOULMATE, LOVER, FRIEND ON THE PATH,
YOU SHOWED ME THAT I COULD CHANNEL
AND YOU AWAKENED MY CONSCIOUSNESS TO
THE TRUE ME.

THANK YOU
I LOVE YOU
MAY ALL YOUR DREAMS COME TRUE!

INTRODUCTION :

This is a little story about how I came to write this book:

I was living in Palo Alto, California in the fall of 1986, playing in a psychedelic rock band called the Random Factor, and going to a number of New Age workshops and gatherings. Suffice to say I was young on my spiritual path and just beginning to realize a whole other world of ideas and alternative realities that existed beyond the pale of normal society. I had done my share of psychedelic drugs in college, and after, and many of the experiences I had would give me glimpses into the true reality behind the illusion; but I hadn't ever come to any very firm realizations for myself as to where I fit in in the great scheme of things.

Most of my understandings of a personal nature had come for me in the process of creation through art, music, writing poetry etc. It was in the state of mind during creation that I could lose my little self for a moment and tune into a greater part of me that seemed to want to come through. The time spent with the band was the crescendo of a wave of personal creativity that began for me in college, and when the band broke up in the fall of 1986 I was ready to explore another part of me that I had never really explored. At this time I started to re-remember a number of skills that I already possessed including massage, crystal healing, tarot reading etc. Also at this time I began to experiment with playing New Age music in the studio, and I made a tape for massage that is now in distribution. Afer six months of exploration I felt I needed a change of residence but I had no idea where to go. A good friend of mine suggested that I go to Lama Foundation in northern New Mexico and use one of their hermitages. I decided to go there for a three day hermitage in May of 1987 and then to return to California to follow the Grateful Dead for at least a year. As it turned out my higher- self had other plans!

I came to Lama Foundation, worked for a week with the community, did my hermitage, came down, and decided to stay for the summer.. The day I arrived at Lama I was asked if I wanted to get stoned with some of the staff; I declined and thus began to release my desire to do drugs. In July I made the connection with my heart partner Areana, and we immediately began to channel information to eachother. We spent the winter together at Lama which was one of the most incredible and most difficult times in my life. As part of an intentional community I was constantly forced to state my truth and declare my intentions; both of which were things I found it difficult to be clear about.

We left Lama in the spring of 1988, came to California to clear up unfinished business, went to Guatemala, followed the Grateful Dead for the summer, and returned to Taos, New Mexico in the fall . In the next two years we created a bed and breakfast, and owned a metaphysical bookstore which we sold in the fall of 1990. We flew to Hawaii and spent the next eight months recuperating and asking for our next step. A number of communities were starting on Kauai and we thought that they must be the reason we were there. In the spring of 1991, however, my tape "Massage Meditation was picked up by a national distributor and I returned to the mainland to market it. We spent the next three months with Areana's parents in Los Angeles trying to get their house sold. At the end of the three months I was totally depressed and suicidal and we left to return to Taos for lack of anything better to do. I felt upon my return that my life had reached a dead end and I couldn't see any way out of my depression but suicide. I went back to my old store and received a psychic reading from an old friend. He told me that I was going to write a book and that it would come through me one chapter at a time. In the dark state I was in I had incredible resistance to this idea, and I drove out to the Rio Grande Gorge Bridge intending to jump off and end my life. When I walked out to the center of the bridge there was a spaceship right there. I made the connection with the ship's crew and they reminded me that I had made the decision to incarnate at this time to help in the planet's transition. They said that I could jump but I would simply come on board their ship and help from the other side. This was due to the commitment I had made when I incarnated, i.e. to stay in service to humanity until the transition was complete. I decided to stay in my body a little longer and to do the book. Each day I wrote one chapter. The book came through me in one month! About half way through I realized I was conversing with a being who was helping me to bring information in from a higher source. When I asked who I was taking to I was given the name of El Morya who is an Ascended Master and one of the guiding members of the White Brotherhood.

I realize now that I needed to write this book for my own personal understanding and evolution. This process is now leading me to my next phase of growth on the path to God. This book is like a guidebook for me to remember and release all my past incarnations on the Earth, and in the Solar System, so that I may move onward towards a reunion with my true identity; a reunion with Spirit. As I mention in the book, now is a good time to get down in some form all the memories and realizations that you have inside of you. If you do this I guarantee you it will lead you foreward on your path to unity with your true self, your cosmic self. If it feels right you can ask the Ascended Masters for help with this.

I hope that you find the material in this book meaningful and useful, and that you share it with your friends on the path when you are done.

May all your dreams come true!

ONE DREAM ONE
TWO BREATHE TWO
THREE DANCE THREE
FOUR EARTH FOUR
FIVE SING FIVE
SIX LOVE SIX
SEVEN SPIRIT SEVEN
EIGHT CLIMB EIGHT
NINE DIVINE NINE

ONE IS ONE AND ONLY ONE * BEGINNING ONE AND ENDING ONE * ALWAYS ONE AND FOREVER ONE * ONE IS TO DREAM AND TO DREAM IS TO BE ONE * ONE WITH ALL AND ONE WITH NONE *

TWO IS TWO AND TWO IS YOU * THE TWO OF THE DREAM AND THE YOU THAT IS BREATH * THE IN-BREATH AND THE OUT-BREATH * THE YOU THAT IS LIFE AND THE YOU THAT IS DEATH *

THREE IS THREE THE THREE OF THE DREAM * THE THREE THAT IS YOU AND THE THREE THAT IS ME * THE THREE IS THE DANCE THAT WE DANCE IN THE DREAM * THE DREAM OF THE LIFE AND THE DEATH OF THE BREATH *

FOUR IS THE FOUR OF THE EARTH IN THE DREAM * AND THE DANCE AND THE BREATH OF THE YOU AND THE ME * AS WE LIVE AND DIE ALONG THE WAY * THE FOUR OF THE EARTH IS THE FOUR THAT WE SEE AS WE DANCE THE ONE THE TWO AND THE THREE *

FIVE IS THE FIVE OF THE DREAM COME ALIVE * TO DANCE AND TO SING OF THE LIFE AND THE DEATH * OF THE ONE AND THE TWO AND THE ME AND THE BREATH * OF THE THREE AND THE FOUR AND THE EARTH THAT WE BLESS *

SIX IS THE SIX IS THE LOVE OF THE DREAM * THAT SPRINGS FROM THE HEART IN THE DANCE AND THE SONG * AND TOUCHES US ALL WITH THE BREATH SO SUBLIME * AS WE FOLLOW THE PATH FROM THE ONE TO THE NINE *

SEVEN IS SPIRIT IN WHICH WE ALL TRUST * TO WATER OUR SOULS AS WE DREAM AND WE BREATHE * AS WE DANCE ON THE EARTH AND SING LOVE TO THE SKY * WE GIVE PRAISE TO SPIRIT THE ALL-SEEING EYE *

EIGHT IS THE EIGHT AND ISN'T IT GREAT * AS YOU RISE TO THE SEVEN YOU SWING THROUGH THE GATE * WITH YOUR FEET ON THE EARTH AND LOVE ON YOUR MIND * SET YOUR EYE ON THE MOUNTAIN AND CLIMB, CLIMB, CLIMB *

NINE IS DIVINE WHERE YOU LEAVE BEHIND YOUR MIND * WHERE THE DREAM FADES AWAY AND YOUR DANCE GETS REAL STILL * THE BREATH AND THE SONG ARE SOFT AS THE BREEZE * AND LIFE AND DEATH ARE JUST MEMORY * BUT THE LOVE THAT IS YOU CONTINUES TO SHINE * FOREVER AND EVER IN THE HEART SO DIVINE *

Today is a One day
a good day for
Dreaming

To dream is to imagine, Image-in, the way things could be. This is the first step in the manifestation process. You can dream consciously or unconsciously, and either kind can manifest itself into physical reality. To consciously dream you must release all need to see your dream manifest, you must become unattatched to any outcome in particular, and you must trust Spirit to bring you what you need for your evolution and destiny.

Unconscious dreaming is when your ego desires a certain outcome, and exerts willpower to create this outcome, whether it is right on a soul-level or not. These dreams come from the first three chakras which channel selfish desires through the agency of the will. When we are still ruled by our ego, and our lower chakra-desires, we manifest dreams that will teach us about survival, sexual energy, and power. We try to manipulate our reality through these three chakra-energies.

Our dreams are usually a combination of the lower energies, and when we use a power to manipulate another being, we invariably find that we are manipulated by another being in return. For each action we take on the ego-level we recieve a similar action in return. This gradually makes us more discriminating in our actions towards others. We begin to desire to help others, so that when we seek help it will be there for us.

Once we begin to dream at the heart-level, we begin to seek ways to manifest our love in the world, and to create dreams that will help the world become a more compassionate and loving place. Many times we seek to create this love through the lower chakras, out of force of habit. Eventually we learn that true love is heart-love, not sexual/survival/power pretending to be love, and that using love in this way is not helpful in our evolution or growth. It is at this point that we begin to actively seek guidance about the higher forms of manifestation, those that are for the good of all, and we actively seek to help others without manipulating them for our own gain. Selfless service is the highest form of dreaming on the planet, and the truth is that all selfless action automatically returns blessings to the server a million times over.

This "principal of return" is why all the world's spiritual teachings speak of doing for others; not because it is good, or right, or expected of a high being, but because this is how we best can learn through our actions. Contrary to the ego-teaching of "get yours while you can", even if you run over everyone else in the process, the upper-chakra dream is to serve everyone according to their needs, and to know that selfless dreaming actually is the most selfish because we are really all one in the greater dream. By serving others, you serve yourself, and all your lessons will be in the form of blessings from others to you in return.

On the highest level, the Earth and the Universe are all a dream created to serve all of God's creatures. The Earth gives of herself, so that all her creations may have someplace to grow and evolve through acting out their personal dreams. It is the Earth's personal dream to serve all her creatures, and she does so selflessly to the point of allowing herself to be defiled and abused by all the lower chakra dreamers among humanity. This may seem strange to those who know the Earth as a conscious being, but it really is the highest form of service. The Earth understands the law of return, and she knows that those who defile her will reap the rewards of bad air, water and food. If you hurt the Earth you only hurt yourself. This is becoming common knowledge now amongst even the densest of humans, and they are beginning to change their ways.

The Earth has great patience with her creations, and when she does react to their excesses it is only after a very long time of waiting for them to change. The Earth only reacts in self-defense of her own existence. The Earth knows that we cannot learn without her body for us to live on, so she takes care of herself. The Earth-changes that have been prophesied by previous dreamers will come to pass in direct proportion to the change in consciousness of Earth's creatures. Earth and her progeny are inseparable.

There is great rejoicing in the upper realms right now as the Earth begins to translate herself from a material being into a being of light. All of her creatures must make this shift as well if they wish to share space with the

Earth in the future. Since material existence is in truth " frozen light", light that has slowed to a crawl, the shift requires an unfreezing of the light to speed us all up into a faster vibration. The freezing of the light provided us a great service: allowing us to see eachother in slow motion. We have been able to analyse what occurs around us in great detail, and this helped us to learn the spiritual laws through the medium of our action, and the observation of others actions, at a slowed pace. This slowing down of the light into physicality has been the greatest gift we have ever recieved, but it is about to end here on the Earth. All of us who have lived and died together, over the eons of "frozen-light-time", must now prepare to unfreeze the light along with the Earth. In this way we may rejoin the realms of light that await us with great appreciation for all we've accomplished. We are the masters of frozen-time, and we will all share our personal understanding of the dream we created when we have unfrozen ourselves, and we join our brothers and sisters in the unbound realms of light.

So rejoice and give yourselves a hand, and lend a hand to those whose ego-self is keeping them from undergoing a shift. We are all truly ready to unfreeze, but some of us have become stuck to the walls, so to speak, and need encouragement to get free from old concepts and understandings created over eons of time. There is no need to force anyone to become unglued, but you can use your personal dream to share with them what is now occuring. Ask the Earth to help you see exactly where they are sticking, and how to speak to their dream, so they will loosen their grip in the way that best suits them. This is important work, as we begin to spin out of time and the Earth-changes accelerate. As all of us begin to loose ourselves from the past this transition time will be very exciting, or very scary, depending on our personal level of release from the "illusion- glue". Any way you can find to talk of what is happening, to share your dream, this is the time to do it. Now is the time to release the gates of "frozen-emotion", "frozen-thought", "frozen-action", to free yourself from the limits of materiality, and to move with the unfreezing glacier of "Earth-time" into the "un-time" of the "liquid-light".

Remember, as you encounter resistance from still-frozen souls, the shift has already happened, and you can always call upon the Earth and your lightguides for protection from the sticky-ones. Remember, it is taking an enormous amount of energy for those still frozen to resist the glacier's melting flow. Those in the flow have begun to tap the infinlte energies of light, and are unstoppable by anyone or anything except themselves. Hear the sound of the glacier cracking, sense the onrushing "liquid-lovelight" pushing all in its path, know the truth of the unfreezing "collective time-dream", feel the pulse of spiritual awakening, touch the consciousness of the newborn Earthmother alive in the lightstream, allow yourself to sense the shifting illusion, and know that you are not alone in your understandings. We are all tasting our future, and it is sweet and fulfilling. Our personal dreams are contacting the creator's dreams and they are the same. We are all one with the light of forever.

Today is a Two Day
a good day for
Breathing

The breath is all-encompassing. Everything that breathes is alive, and everything is alive. The breath is the pulse of Spirit into and out of creation. It is the source of all life.

The in-breath, or inspiration, is the activator that moves the inanimate creation to be born anew each moment. The out breath, or expiration, releases Spirit from the creation to fly back to the Creator, whose Divine breath is the source of all inspiration. This is the cycle, or pulse, of creation; the Divine circuit that animates reality continuously with the inspiration of the Divine. This is the never-ending source of all that gives us life.

Nothing in the material, and non-material, reality would exist without this breath pulsing in and out, completing the circuit of creative electricity that animates all forms. We are all electric cells constantly recharging, and discharging, as we move through our environment. Our environment is also breathing the Divine breath, and we share energy every moment we are alive. This breath is what joins us with the whole of creation. If we place our consciousness on our breath, we can become aware of the connection, and share awareness with anything we wish to, at any time. The breath carries the whole of creation with it as it moves, and we can become aware of the knowledge of the Universe simply by consciously breathing in the Divine awareness. As a matter of fact this is all we truly are, the breath of God. This is how we know all we know, how we know ourselves and eachother. We think that we know something through our minds but this is illusion. All we know is aquired through our connection with the Divine breath. We literally breathe eachother every moment we are alive and, therefore, we are constantly connected to the awareness of everything. If we desire the answer to any question, we simply must breathe into the question, and on the inspiration the knowledge will arrive. It is up to us to hear the answer, but it is always there when we place our consciousness upon it. It is the same for anything we wish to know about our environment. We simply must breathe with whatever it is we desire to understand, and the knowledge will be there on the incoming breath.

This principal is why so many spiritual disciplines focus on purifying the breath. Everything we know is filtered, through who we are, via the breath. As we breathe, the knowledge enters our being and encounters all our preconceptions, beliefs, and understandings. The more open and un-conceived we are about everything, the greater our ability to gain knowledge through the breath. This is the great paradox of our existence. We believe that we must accumulate, and store, knowledge if we are to understand anything. But the truth is; we must become completely empty of all previous thoughts, beliefs, and understandings if we are to receive true awareness from the Divine. All is available at each moment of inspiration, so there is no need to store anything at any time. We can simply breathe in and know it when the moment arises. Anything we accumulate simply blocks the true understanding, and replaces it with what we think we know. Since knowledge is not fixed, we will miss out on the latest version from the source if we replace it with our outdated beliefs. This can severely limit our growth and evolution, causing us to get stuck in a never-ending cycle of living in "past-story".

If we purify the breath, by emptying ourselves of what we think we know, we will constantly be inspired with the Divine breath, and we will know all there is to know at any time we desire to know it. This is the high spiritual truth from the eons of time, and we can decide at any time to join with those souls who have breathed with God, or we can stay with the old preconceptions and miss out on all the latest Divine inspiration. The choice, as always, is ours.

Today is a Three day
a good day for
Dancing

To dance, to flow with the eternal movement of the cosmos, is the highest expression of humanity,. Everything in the created world is in constant motion; flowing in and out of eachother in an endless series of interactions that never exactly repeat themselves. As we dance our dream, to the song of the spheres, we move to the beat and rhythm of our own atomic and molecular structure. This is the way we are meant to be; listening to the rhythm of the cosmos, and matching our flow with the beat of life. Just as we can know everything through the breath, we can also fuse our consciousness with all the levels of reality, through matching our dance with whatever we wish to join.

If you spend a lot of time in nature, you can become sensitive to each plant's particular flow, and each insect's dance with the Divine. You can know in advance what a wild animal will do next, or when a storm is coming up, all through the dance of the particles of creation. To do these things, you must become very quiet inside yourself in order to hear the tiny nuances of movement as particles interact on the subtlest of levels. Then you must pay very close attention to what occurs after the signal has been given. This precognizance is on a denser level than psychic attunement, so you must open all the senses and feel the elements merging with your aura. The motion will contact your aura first, and then it will begin to connect with the pulsing of your breath and body. If you make the breath very subtle, and heighten the attentiveness of your skin, you will begin to be aware of the tiniest signals from nature. Practice sitting next to a tree and projecting yourself into its trunk. Become the sap, the roots, and the leaves. If you can become aware of their motion, their internal and external dance, you will be fine-tuned enough to begin interacting with the elementals that inhabit the most subtle of nature's realms.

The elementals are the intelligences one step up from the elements of

physical reality. They are the building blocks of nature. These intelligences, through their dance, awaken the dance and dream in
each of the Earth's creations, setting them in motion, and maintaining a space for them to thrive and evolve. These elementals are the Divine gardeners of Earth, connecting both with the Creator and the Earthmother to shape the movement of the natural realms. We too are connected with both the Divine and the Earth. Our original dispensation on the Earth was to shepherd, name, and befriend the rest of the kingdom of nature. Because of this dispensation from the Divine, our bodies have been created to be receivers for Divine inspiration, and as communication vehicles for the emparting of this information to our brothers and sisters on the Earth. We were asked, in the very beginning times, to come here in spirit form and aid the elementals in creating the dance of life on this beautiful planet Earth. All the creatures of Earth look to us for guidance and friendship, and for their identity. Without us the animal and other forms are lacking in the ability to connect fully with the Divine inspiration that flows from the dance of the cosmos. In this time of transition, it is being asked of us to remember our brother and sister creations, and to work with the Earth to help them connect with the Divine's constant nurturing advice and love. Many humans are now realizing this connection and working together to help their friends through this transitory shift in Earth consciousness.

As you attune yourself to the Divine dance, and begin to dance your own personal dream, you will find yourself releasing many of your previous belief systems, and your structured existence, and desiring to spend more and more time in nature. This is only the natural course of events for those of us ready to make the shift to "spirit-centered" living. We are ready to reconnect with our original purpose on the Earth, but it will be on a higher level of compassion, and understanding, than we have experienced up until now. Our incarnation in bodies, and the subsequent blocking of our spiritual abilities, was all part of the Divine plan. This allowed us to lose our spiritual arrogance long enough to gain the insight necessary to bring the whole of creation to spirit awareness. This was not possible in the beginning when we were in our light bodies, and we had no experience with the difficulties of understanding that would arise once we donned our physical shells. Now we have been through the darkness, feeling disconnected from our source, and unable to keep a clear connection with the inspirational flow of "spirit-truth". Now as we dance our dream, and open to the constant flow of life, we can reconnect with nature, and bring our brothers and sisters with us to the next stage of creation, where we all match our dance with the dance of the Divine.

So attune yourselves to the motion that surrounds you, and begin to see the pattern that nature provides us for interpreting the Divine message. Begin to reconnect with the elementals, who have never lost their link to nature, and ask them for insight and help in connecting to any specific plant, animal or insect you feel drawn to flow with. Open your senses to the wind and the rain, and begin to appreciate the flow of the Earth's weather; to understand the role it plays as the nurturer of all of creation on the Earthmother. Most of all attune yourself to the Earth herself, and ask what part you might play in the rediscovery of our dispensation as stewards of the kingdom of nature. Through the Earth you will find the dance that creates your dream, and links you to the dreams of the cosmos. As you dance in the flow, and become inspired, you will get glimpses of the future that is coming, of the grand design. As the glimpses come, try and put them in some form, perhaps a dance or song, so that others may discover their part to play and begin to dance their dream.

Never doubt that you too are a Divine dreamer, dancing on the flow of inspired lightwaves, attuned to the rhythm of the whole of creation, and connected with your brothers and sisters as we dance in the new tomorrow each moment of our lives.

Today is a Four day
a good day for working
with the Earth

THE EARTH
BORN FROM THE DREAM OF THE ONE
THE BREATH AND SONG OF
THE DIVINE

THE EARTH
CONSECRATED BY THE SELFLESS
SOUL-DREAMERS WHO
SING THE DREAM
AWAKE

THE EARTH
HER GLORY COMPLETE AS A
NURTURER OF DREAMING
SOULS
NOW REJOICES IN
THE FREEDOM FROM HER
TASK

THE EARTH
MAINTAINED BY THE DANCE OF THE
DREAMWEAVERS, YOU AND I
WHO BELIEVE IN THE
DREAM

THE EARTH
IS IN CONTROL OF HER
DESTINY
HER SOUL-URGE IS
STRONG AND PURE
TO RELEASE THE
DREAM

THE EARTH
SO LONG AGO
MADE UP HER
MIND
TO BREAK FREE FROM HER
BONDS
AND SOAR AS A
STAR

Let me tell you a story:

In the beginning times, before the dream was more than a thought bubbling up from the tides of the Divine mind, before the Universe had begun its long spin out from the All-Knowing's eye, before the myriad forms had coalesced from the ethereal emanations surrounding the Central Sun, long, long ago from the vantagepoint we assume now, there occurred a ripple in the still pool of eternity; a ripple whose source is still a mystery, and whose purpose and direction is shrouded to all except the ultimate perceiver, God.

Now this ripple in the unformed was quite small really, just a point of motion that quickly subsided, as if the effort to move the eternal was too immense to last more than a beat in un-time, but the effect of this ripple, coming as it did in the beginning of all beginnings, was enormous, and seemingly unstoppable, reverberating in the canyons of forever up until this very day.

Now it is very possible that the ripple was part of the plan, and was placed there by God for purposes that will become clear in the fullness of time, but it is equally possible that the ripple was a random occurrence, unforeseen by the creator, a randomness that has had a greater effect on the Universe and all its realms than perhaps anything else.

Now if we go back to the beginning, and follow the Universe as it spins out from the All-Seeing eye, we perceive the higher, more ethereal realms in formation; realms that will form the cosmic blueprint for other levels of creation; and here we see the Ripple-Effect butting its head in in the persona of Lucifer.

Lucifer was an angel of unequaled beauty. So bright a star was never seen before his coming, and never seen since. In the fiery moments of Lucifer's birth from the Central Sun, all the light from the Divine seemed to pass to Lucifer, so that the Creator's light dimmed and wavered, blinking on and off for several moments as it discharged across the gap to light the first star.

Now Lucifer's creation being the first of its kind, the Divine had nothing to compare it to, and for the moment, as the Creator contemplated creation, all seemed well. But looking back we can see that the ripple had penetrated the space around the Central Sun, causing the exchange of light and energy in the first creation to pulse on and off, draining the Creator's light more than was necessary or planned for. The ripple also had penetrated the light itself so that Lucifer, though brighter than any other, had a rippling on the edge of his being, and his light shone on and off instead of constantly on like the Divine's light.

After awhile the Creator noticed this unusual pulsing effect, and it was quite beautiful to watch, the irregularity causing all the infinite colors that make up light to show themselves on the edge of Lucifer's being. It was truly a glorious show.

After contemplating his creation, the Divine desired to create more beings of light, and did so, but none matched the intensity, brilliance, and beauty of the first. Some creations had the ripple, and shone their colors, others were constant in their light, though very dim compared to the Divine.

As the Creator brought forth his stars Lucifer began to be conscious of what was occurring, and as he watched he tried to mimic the creation as he perceived it. After a while he was successful in producing a small light, that was very colorful but also very dim, and like its creator it rippled continuously on its edges. For a long time the Creator sat and contemplated creation and Lucifer watched his creation as well. As this was happening a curious thing occurred. The stars/angels with the ripple-effect in them began to move away from those with constant light, and also away from the Creator, and towards Lucifer. Once again the ripple had come into play, causing a wave of ripples that interacted with all those angels with rippling edges, and creating a force or motion through this interaction. Those beings with constant light were unaffected by the ripple-wave, though they were able to perceive its effect on the others. After a period of un-time, Lucifer, his creation, and the rippled angels had moved far away, and the Divine and his constant angels were aware of them as a long string of colored lights spiraling away in the distance.

At this point the Creator made an effort to contact Lucifer, and tried to bring the angels back, but the ripple-wave broke up the lightwave he sent into a long arc of color bands that was truly beautiful to see but lacked the energy focus to bring the angels back. The Creator did manage to send a message along the color-bow, that he and the constant angels would get together their light and make another effort to retrieve Lucifer's angels, before the bow broke up into tiny color ripples and the connection was lost.

Now, as Lucifer and his band of angels rode the ripple-wave outward, they came to a place that felt very different than where they had been born. This place seemed quite dark, and they noticed that their colors dimmed so much that they couldn't shine their colors across the gaps between them very well. There was also quite a bit of turbulence caused by the ripple-wave bouncing off of some unseen barrier, rippling back at them , and then encountering more oncoming ripples. The angels found themselves caught in various undertows, riptides, and whirlpools which separated them from eachother. This caused quite a few of the angels to become lost , and the rest to become confused and disoriented.

Lucifer, being the first and brightest angel, immediately recognized that they were at the edge of creation, and that if he and his creation were to survive they must bring everyone back together at once. Therefore, Lucifer grabbed his creation in a very tight grip, and he began to spin very rapidly, shining as brightly as he could against the oppressive darkness. One by one the angels that were still close also began to spin and shine as Lucifer did, and they found as they did so their light grew much stronger, and their ability to withstand the ripples' force was greater. Though they couldn't get any closer to Lucifer, or to eachother, they didn't seem to move any farther away. It seems that their spinning created a counterforce to the ripple-waves, and ripple-tides, that allowed them to maintain their position and conserve their light. Thus, here at the edge of creation, Lucifer and the rippled angels formed an outpost of light, and over time brought forth their own creations from the light of their beings. These creations, although very dim, were all very beautiful and colorful, and each was totally unique. These created-ones rippled and spun like their creators, and they stayed quite close to their creator-stars in order to share their light, and to be taught the mysterious and wonderful story of creation.

Eventually, after a long time of creating and teaching the planets/created-ones, the angels settled down to rest, and they contemplated all they had wrought. The planets then took over the job of creating, bringing forth all sorts of wondrous lifeforms out of the essence of their beings. Once again, each of these lifeforms spun and rippled its unique colors to creation and stayed very close to its creator-being/planet. Both the planets and lifeforms shared the light of their particular star/angel. These lifeforms had very little light of their own, and they depended on the angel/planet matrix to survive. Many lifeforms couldn't survive at all and were reabsorbed back into their host planet. Eventually some of the individual lifeforms managed to join together what light they had, and they noticed that by joining they were able to reproduce themselves. Gradually these larger lifeforms spread out all over their host planets and interacted with the other lifeforms. They found that they learned from these interactions, and some of the lifeforms learned to use what they found around them to create forms that could be used for more interesting interactions with eachother and their environment.

One of the more interesting ripple-effects that came into play, at about this time, was the effect of time. Because the rippled creation did not have constant light, their appearance was always changing, never quite repeating itself. Since each angel had been set apart from the others by the tides at the edge of creation, and each one was unique, each angel's creation was also unique and separate from the other angels' creation. The constant flow of the ripple-waves forced each star to spin and expend energy to keep its position, and this kept the angels from joining eachother. Once a star began its spin, following Lucifer's lead, it then followed its own rhythm of creation, and becoming absorbed in the creative process became unaware of anything else. Lucifer's creation had happened at the very beginning of their journey, before any spinning had occurred to start the clocks of time in motion. So relative to Lucifer the other angels' creations were younger, while Lucifer's creation played the role of elder to the rest of creation.

Now Lucifer's creation had the most light of any of the planets, and therefore its lifeforms had more light than any other lifeforms. SInce Lucifer was the main light source for both his planet, and his planet's lifeforms, they all considered Lucifer their supreme creator, and kept alive the story of his miraculous actions at the edge of creation that had saved them from becoming lost. Now, evcn Lucifer, as bright and as strong as he was, could not bridge the gap to the other angels, and this was very frustrating for him. Accordingly he encouraged the lifeforms of his planet to grow and create in his name, and, after a very long time, the dominant lifeform on Lucifer's creation came to posess the ability to create a useful form that could bridge the gap to the other stars. Lucifer was extremely happy about this and he urged the lifeforms to travel to the nearest angel, and inform him and his creation of what they had discovered. Thus began the journeys of Lucifer's children to the lessser creation, encouraging other lifeforms to evolve and grow until they too could travel between the stars.

Meanwhile, back at the Central Sun, the Divine and his constant angels had joined their energies in an attempt to contact the rippled angels and bring them back to the center of creation. The creator and his angels sent out a very brilliant ray of light that was very focused. This ray managed to bridge the distance to the edge of creation, and it carried a message of love from the Divine, and a desire to have the rippled ones come home. Unfortunately, the strong spin of the rippled angels repulsed the beam of focused light, sending it off into space before it could reach their consciousness. It did, however, pass through the planets on its way out, affecting certain of the lifeforms there, and it contacted one of the lost angels which had never learned to spin. This angel received the message, and was carried back to the center of creation on the beam of light. On its return to the center, this lost angel related what it remembered of its journey to the edge, incuding its interaction with the ripples. It also described what it had perceived at the edge of creation itself, but this part was understandably confused.

The Divine and his angels were exerting quite a bit of energy to keep the rippled angel close to them, so they decided to send him back as a messenger to the other rippled angels. The messenger returned to the edge of creation on the beam of light to deliver the Divine message of love, and the Creator's desire to have Lucifer and the other angels return to the center as soon as possible on the beam of light. When the messenger returned to the edge of creation he saw a breathtaking sight. The lesser creation was in full swing, and shining, spinning stars and planets filled the darkness with cascading lights of all colors, shapes and variety. The messenger was stunned by what he saw, and was quite unable to comprehend it. " How could this be possilbe?", he thought as he approached Lucifer and his planet. Once again, however, the beam of light was repulsed, but as the messenger was flung away from Lucifer, he passed through Lucifer's creation and picked up an inkling of what might have occurred from one of the lifeforms. This lifeform had encountered the first beam of light and managed to get the gist of its message. Now, as the beam came through a second time, the messenger latched onto the thoughts of the lifeform, and he discovered the story of Lucifer's miraculous actions that had saved these lifeforms from certain extinction. As the messenger flashed by, he got off a quick message to this lifeform that the Divine loved him, and would like to bring him home on the beam of light as soon as possible. Then the messenger was flung out into space, and began the return journey to the center, with the hope that his message was received and Lucifer would be ready when the next beam came by.

On returning to the center, the messenger informed the Divine of his actions, and told him the story of the lesser creation garnered from the lifeform on Lucifer's creation. All of this puzzled the Divine greatly, and he sat and pondered, and mused and sat, for a very long time, until the constant ones became alarmed at his lack of attention to them. Finally, the Creator came out of his reverie and made a decision, a decision that like the ripple would echo through the ages for a very long time. The Creator decided to send his constant angels on a mission to Lucifer, and to the lesser creation, to see if a way could be found to counteract the ripple-effect and bring the whole of Lucifer's creation back to the central sun. So the messenger and the constant angels rode the lightwave back to the edge of creation, and the Divine promised to keep the channel open, so that anyone that desired could ride the wave back to him at any time.

Thus began a mission that would continue for eons, up until the present day in fact....but that is another story.

Today is a Five day
a good day for
Singing

When you sing your whole body vibrates from your head to your toes. This vibration releases negative emotions that are stuck in your body, and at the same time brings you positive feelings of love, harmony and oneness with everything. It is almost impossible to be angry while you are singing, and it is hard not to feel better about everything after you have stopped.

Many people who are clairaudient hear a constant singing of the angels and nature spirits as they go about their work on the Earth. This constant singing sets up a wave of harmonic vibration around the singer, that repulses any harmful thought patterns, and creates a calm, peaceful, harmonious environment wherever the singer goes.

Because sound is vibration, and creates a waveform, it has been credited by all the world's spiritual masters as the initial impetus in the formation of the Universe. All of creation vibrates and forms a wave. Each of us is a moving, vibrating waveform. Like the breath, and the dance, it is possible for each of us to attune our vibration to the rest of creation, harmonizing our song with nature, angels, nature spirits and the whole of the Universe. When we begin to sing our song in harmony with the Universe we enter the cosmic flow, our wave meets with no resistance, and we become a healing force for ourselves and our environment on the Earth.

Vibrational, energetic healing is now using toning to release blocks in the body. Theoretically this sounding work could heal any disease, because each disease has its own unique vibration and wave form. Attunement to the unique wave of the disease, and toning into it with the correct vibration, will set up an interference pattern and cancel the disease wave out. This is one of the medicines of the future. As well, each color has its own vibration, and is a wave of light. Color therapy is essentially the singing of color into a person's aura to attune it, helping the person's individual wave to move into harmony with the flow of the cosmos.

A long, long time ago, when we were spirit without bodies, we sang of the love of creation, and through our song brought our world into form. The angels and the elementals continue this work today, singing the love for all beings as they move from plant, to insect, to animal, to human, creating the conditions necessary for life, growth, and evolution on the Earth. Scientific thought and technology have tried to disavow the work of these beings, and even alter it for their own purposes, declaring that we are on our own, can destroy nature, and still live. This is false understanding as they shall soon see. Humanity is on the brink of rediscovering its true purpose on Earth, which is to co-create with the Divine singers; the angels and elementals. We will soon begin to create a new world of forms through singing it into being.

The angels are actively contacting all of us who are attuned to co-creating with them at this time, and we will be ready when the Earth decides she's had enough of the materialists, and she begins to release them to their own fate. Those who are disconnected from the life giving singing of the angels will not last an hour in their bodies without the Divine support they have always received. Their bodies cannot sustain themselves in the world without a strong connection to the source through these intermediaries, and they will begin to self-destruct as rampant disease is given full reign. They will literally vibrate themselves into nothingness.

Now is the time to match your particular song, breath, and dance with the Creator's and to connect with the angels and elementals that are your body's lifesource. Learn from them how to sing yourself into harmony, to flow with the eternal cosmic inspiration, and we will all co-create the new world into form together!

Today is a Six day
a good day for
Love

Love is the cosmic glue, the fiber of the Universe, the sap that joins us all as one big family. Love is contained in the light of the creator. It is the message encoded in the light of God that states, "You are all one with me", " All is perfect in my eyes", " You are all protected, perfect, immortal", "You are all loved".

As each of us makes the journey, from the source to the Earth, we sometimes get lost from the message; we feel trapped, alone, without love. It is then that the Creator sends us a messenger, one who speaks and acts as a channel for the Creator's light. Slowly, with their guidance, we begin to remember who we are, LOVE, where we came from, THE SOURCE, and that we are always one with and connected to the message of love.

In the dream world we live in now, the illusion of reality is created and maintained by the angels and elementals through their song of love. They are beings of light and love and they cannot do anything but love unconditionally. Their only purpose is to love everything, and through their song of love to maintain the illusion, so that we may evolve and grow on the Earth.

In the beginning times, we all maintained a conscious connection with both the source and the lovelight beings, and we praised them for their contribution to our great experiment of living in illusion. Over time, most of us lost this conscious connection, as we became separated from the source of love, and felt trapped in the illusion we had created. Still, many kept in touch with the angels and elementals, and brought the message from the Creator that was delivered through their song. After a while, even these connections became less and less common, until each autonomous group of humans began to rely on only one individual to make the connection, and bring back a message.

This was the beginning of mystery schools, priesthoods, shamanic sects etc. The majority gave their power of connecting with source away to a few individuals, and then made demands that were unrealistic when they didn't like the message. Throughout all this, the angels and elementals struggled to do their work without our conscious participation. They worked to keep our bodies alive, even when we abused them in an unconscious attempt to be released from the hellish illusion that we'd created. This was the advent of disease on Earth, as well as warfare, murder, suicide etc.

Throughout, the Creator's message of love attempted to manifest in the world, through embodying in beings that had kept a connection open, and who were wondering why everyone else seemed to either be killing eachother or dying. These souls began to separate themselves from the rest of humanity, as much for self-preservation as to make it easier to keep the connection open. The fearful masses, sensing that they were being abandoned in their torment, sought out these angelic humans, and killed them when they could.

It was at this point that the Creator called away his angels to a council, and the elementals were left alone in the enormous task of maintaining the illusion for humanity. Despite their loving nature, this distressed the elementals so much that they purposely hid themselves from humanity, and ignored their pleas for help. They concentrated their energies instead on the plants, insects, and animals. Humanity was unable to maintain itself for long without this important source of love, and so degenerated into mass warfare and genocide, while plagues swept the Earth, wiping out those humans who were fortunate enough not to be killed by their own kind.

As you might have guessed this was just before the deluge, and it went on for some time. Meanwhile, the Creator and the angels councilled, and decided a clean slate was the answer. So the angels returned, and prepared for the flood that would cleanse the world of all that was not loving. Many of the angels, , upon their return, were truly shocked at the state of the world, and chided the elementals, who became even more upset and retreated to the farthest reaches of the planet to escape from it all.

Now, each of the angels had a group of humans they were responsible for, and though they knew that the whole Earth should be cleansed, they felt sorry for humanity. Thus each secretly decided to save a few of the more connected beings. Therefore, all the Noahs of the world, and there were many, were contacted and saved from certain destruction. Unfortunately, their offspring often were ensouled by reincarnating spirits, of the fearful / unconnected type, who had died in the flood. This caused the cycle to repeat itself all over again, all the way up until the present day.

This brings us back to the topic of the day, love. Currently the energy of love has been increased substantially on Earth, and more and more souls are beginning to reconnect with the angels, elementals, and the source itself. As we all do this, all the memories of the past are flooding into our consciousness so that we can begin to release the fear, and reconnect with the Divine message encoded in the light. As we release the fear, and begin to understand where our attatchment to the dream made us fearful, we can start to vision a new way of living. We can imagine being reconnected to the elementals, to the plants, insects, and animals, to the angels and the Creator. We can decide to all be messengers of love to eachother, so that the whole of creation resounds with the same song, dances the same dance of perfection, harmony, beauty, truth, understanding, and of course love. The whole process we've been through, of being lost, alone, separate, and unconscious, has brought us to this moment of cosmic a-tone-ment. By going our own way for a while, we realized our interdependence as creatures of light and love. Now, we must thrust away the vestiges of unloving thought and action that cloud the horizon, and accept the truth of who we are. No longer can we be content to be trapped in an illusion, the one we created in the first place, and a place none of us wants to be in. No longer can we pretend that this is all there is for us. We must move beyond the boundaries caused by hate, greed, injustice, and violence, and begin to see that we are the ones that create it all. We can choose! The angels, the elementals, and the Creator await our answer as the song of love is brought to a ringing crescendo that no one can fail to hear. No one can claim any longer that they didn't hear the message of love that impregnates each atom, and each particle of existence.

Love is in the air we breathe, and the water we drink. It is in the dreams we dream, and the words we speak. It is everpresent, and the message is perfectly clear. Remember your source, accept your Divinity, celebrate your oneness, sing praises of love to all you see, become one with your dreams, for now is the time of love on Earth!

Today is a Seven day
a good day for
connecting with
Spirit

Spirit is actively coming onto the Earth at this time, to help bring in new energy, new ideas, and new forms into manifestation. It is important for those beings who can hear the voice of Spirit, to try and put down what they hear, in whatever form seems most appropriate. Artists, musicians, writers, and dancers have been doing this throughout time. But now, for the first time since the beginning time, energies are consciously being amped up by the light beings who have incarnated on the planet. This has caused the aura of the planet to expand and reflect the light of Spirit more directly, while simultaneously blocking any negative forces, not already on the planet, from penetrating to the Earth. Also, many light beings are gathering together at points on the earth that are key node/vortex points. This is allowing Spirit to ground into the Earth, by creating a light grid that is transforming the physical forms and not just the mental ones ruled by Earth's aura. This is one reason we see humanity's structural systems in disarray all over the planet. For the last four years, since harmonic convergence, the mental energies have been transformed, causing even the densest beings to have visions and to speak about: " a thousand points of light ", " a new world order ", "perestroika ", " glasnost ", etc.

With the last major node point being grounded at the Great Pyramid in January 1992, these visions will have come down to Earth. This is why there is such chaos on the Earth right now, as the old forms are being forced out through the lens of public scrutiny. From the largest organizational forms, i.e. governments, corporations, secret societies etc., to the smallest atom, all things are being dissolved in consciousness so that the new can emerge in its place. This is the reason so much seems in limbo, and why so many projects fall apart, or appear to be on hold. Nothing new can be created until the old forms, down to the smallest particle of physical reality, are dissolved. As well, all the beings involved in any important project, must have gone through this death process internally if their project is to allign with Spirit fully.

Many beings are beginning, or in the midst of, this process right now, and they will need help to transit this psychic/emotional/physical inner death without leaving the planet. Many will leave in the next few years who are not ready to die to Spirit; including many of the so called leaders of old Earthforms who refuse to change and be Spirit-directed. This may cause chaos in those areas of the Earth that have not created the means for easy transition to new Spirit-directed leadership, i.e. the Soviet Union. Remember, however, that all is being taken care of, at the highest levels, to ensure that humanity does not destroy itself in its process of change.

Many light beings have chosen to actively force change at the most dense and materialistic organizations, and these beings may appear, for awhile, to be the object of persecutions and witch hunts. This is all in the plan, and these souls have chosen their path perfectly. It is helpful to send light and love to help these pioneers, but know that they will prevail in their struggle no matter how bleak it seems. Remember, nothing that is not Spirit-directed will survive this transition. Nothing!

This next period, from now through 1996, will require great patience from those light beings still working in the old systems. These beings will need to guard against becoming too identified with their work, while at the same time staying tied in enough to bring in new energies as they come through. These lightworkers are put where they are mostly to balance the densest ones, and they will need to take alot of personal time with Spirit to avoid burnout and identification with the lesser evolved ones around them. Spirit is actively seeking to ground places of spiritual retreat, and means of resourcing, that are accessible to these working warriors of light. Anything that can help these souls stay tuned to Spirit is needed at this time, and will be supported at the highest levels.

As for those beings outside the old system, they can begin, after January 1992, to bring in the newest forms to those geographical locations that have been purified by Spirit, and are ready to receive the newness of Spirit's light in manifest form. Art, Music, Dance, and Writing will be the forerunners of this attunement to Spirit, but the denser forms will also begin to be replaced from 1992-1996. This depends particularly on the internal changes made by the humans who inhabit the areas in transition. If a critical mass have made the shift to being Spirit-centered, then external forms can begin to shift as well. Humanity is the agent of Spirit in this transition.

These regions, or " Cities of Light ", are beginning to come into their own now, and they will need to be ready to accept the new forms Spirit seeks. They must also be willing to allow visitations from denser souls, who need to connect with the higher vibrations for help in transitioning to Spirit-centeredness. Many of these cities have already become pilgrimage points for the light warriors to resource, and this will continue for the next period, until the energy becomes too quick for materialistic souls to enter. At this point many of the urban light warriors will move permanently to the light cities, and the denser cities will dissolve into the chaos on their own.

As for the prophecies in the bible and elsewhere, these must come to pass, but those living in the light cities will not experience the fullness of the violence and chaos because their energies will be focused at a different vibration. Only those beings who have resisted the shift to Spirit-centeredness, from 1992-1996, will find their external reality a reflection of the inner chaos that reigns when materialism is the inner motivation. Those who do not, or cannot, trust Spirit will be forced to trust the great liars of the age; greed, self-centeredness, force, injustice, hate, etc. These beings will exist for a short time in a world ruled by the forces of darkness and illusion, without any counterbalance of love and light. This will be a moment of Hell on Earth, created to cause the choice to become absolutely clear to those unwilling to choose on their own. To the beings caught in this web of darkness, it will seem that the world is dying, but, as we know, it already has died to make way for the new. To those souls living in this hell, there at first may not seem to be any choices, no way out, but if they allow for the possibility, and strive to hear Spirit's voice, they will be transported out of the illusion. The key will be for them to completely rely on Spirit for their redemption. Many of these souls will experience a Second-Coming of Christ, as in the prophecies, and will feel rewarded by their faith. This is all part of the plan to help free these souls from their delusion, and to cause them to seek Spirit actively in their further incarnations. These beings will be transported to another dimension of existence, after the collapse of the darkness is complete. At that point the cities of light will spread across the newly formed Earth, and Spirit's creations will fill the whole of this part of creation.

Today is an Eight day
a good day to
climb to the
Divine

Once you reach a place of Spirit-centeredness, where Spirit guides whatever it is you do, you find yourself waiting on Spirit to move you wherever you're most useful, or most needed. This requires a great deal of patience, and the ability to release all the needs, urges, and desires of the ego, which invariably gets bored and restless with its lack of attention. The ego believes it has lost its power, when Spirit takes over, and it comes up with visions of death, doom, and gloom, which it sends to the mind in an effort to scare the mind enough that it will decide to act, to do something now. If the mind acts on its own, it will find that whatever it does eventually leads to disaster, and it will have to rationalize its behavior to make it seem o.k.

Now that Spirit has come to Earth in a big way, all ego-centered activity is doomed to immediate failure. The ego is beginning to realize this, as it watches all its favorite forms and structures dissolve in front of its eyes. This external death, of the externalized ego, is forcing the ego inside, to confront its fears of uselessness, powerlessness, and total annihilation. It is very important for all of us to cultivate the ability to see with a spiritual eye. This allows us the understanding of the reason why all the ego's forms keep dissolving. This inner knowing helps to reduce the emotional fear reaction in our bodies, which have been ruled by the ego for all of our present life, and most of our past lives. So as you look out at your ego-world rapidly disintegrating to make way for Spirit's vision to manifest, try and see it through Spirit's eyes. Ask for guidance from Spirit for this, and allow this inner vision to show you what the ego-form will be replaced with. This is one way you will reduce the fear in your body, and your mind will get a glimpse of the new future, which will reduce its anxiety around the dissolving of the only world it knows.

As you begin to perceive your world in Spirit's way, you begin to climb above the chaotic, ego-centered existence, and you begin to get perspective on all that you observe in your own life, and in others' lives.

World events take on new meaning, and things that in the past may have frightened you, or angered you, or made you feel hopeless, will now be seen as the external dissolving of a materialistic world under the cleansing ray of Spirit.

It is important for you to spend as much of your time as possible with other souls who are able to see in this way. That way your ego can't get too much encouragement in its personal view of the world. Spend some time with those souls who are beginning the shift in consciousness, so that you can help them to see what you see, but allow them their own process in the climb from fear into the light.

Spirit is everywhere on the planet now, and accelerating its frequency exponentially. In the next few years it is going to take enormous amounts of energy to keep ego/fear/survival/materialistic forms alive, and it will be necessary, before the end of 1996, to move to the safe havens of the light cities to avoid the possibly violent and chaotic self-destruction of the old forms. There is no need to put yourself in harm's way once you have made the Spirit shift. It will not be helping those who need to shift themselves, and may need the strongest possible choices to help them do so. It is going to be especially difficult if some of these denser beings are your relatives, but you must turn and be with your true spiritual family at this time, to support and vision with Spirit on the new forms of the new world. Remember that all beings are in the perfect place, doing the perfect thing, and they will all shift eventually. You cannot push them into a shift, but they may affect your ability to be present and available to Spirit. The choice is always yours, of course, but meditate on what is best for you, and the new world you're creating, and Spirit will show you the best way to serve at this time.

The climb to the Divine is happening to each of us, and the timing is always a personal one, dependent on ego-resistance and attatchment to things of the past, forms of the past, and relationships of the past. If you can completely release the past, and be in the present, with no attatchment to anything or anyone, then you are ready to become inspired with the light that is beaming upon us all right now. This light will guide you to each successive step upon your personal ladder to the

Divine, and it will seem effortless because “you” are not doing anything. You are simply allowing Spirit to move you, and this brings an enormous relief to the body and mind, which have carried you to this place. They will now be able to rest from the duties they assumed, duties they were not meant to assume in the first place!

In a balanced soul, Spirit informs the body, which moves accordingly, while the mind watches, learns from, and appreciates the movement. This is the basis of Spirit-directed living, and we are all moving in this direction in our lives. As we catch ourselves trying to force something, or make something happen, we can see the ego in action, and if we slowly breathe until the desire to do anything leaves us, tune into Spirit, and ask for our next step, we will begin to flow with the Divine. Eventually, we will be so in the flow, that the asking will cease, and we will simply move with the grace of Spirit, toward whatever is most needed or useful in this time of transition. Remember, under Spirit's guidance, all things are possible and there are no limits. So dream big, and ask for help to manifest your dreams. Then become unattatched to the outcome, remain in the present, and allow your dream to unfold naturally and effortlessly through the wisdom and guidance of the all-knowing, all-seeing inner eye.

Today is a Nine day
perfect for all things
Divine

" The Divine in all things, and all things in the Divine ". This is the first principle in spiritual mastery. To see, hear, think, feel, know, etc., that everything that exists, on all levels of existence, is an expression of the Divine impulse; which is constantly expressing itself in an infinite variety, so as to know itself better through that expression. The more caught up we are in the externalized ego-reality, and the more attatched we are to anything that happens outside ourselves, the more difficult it is to appreciate this Divine truth. The first step toward Divine recognition, literally re-knowing ourselves, is to begin to appreciate and understand all that we are. To do this, we must begin to spend some real time with only ourself, asking questions like, "Who am 1?', "Why am I here?", "Where is here, exactly? ", etc. At first, you may find that the answers come easy, but they are probably expressions of your external reality, and not the true you. For example, you are not your job title, you are not any of your relationships, you are not just a body with a brain, etc.

Now comes the paring down. As you realize what you are not, you have the opportunity to release those identifcations with the external, and find the true you. As you find the true you, underneath those unwanted selves, the desire will be to label yourself anew, "I am a seeker of spiritual truth", "I am a star-soul from Orion", etc. This is only natural, because we are used to identifying ourselves to the outside world, so they may understand who we are. As a matter of fact, modern humanity labels everything, and anything unlabeled is bound to be forgotten. We don't want to be forgotten so we label ourselves, and the labels get more and more subtle as we journey toward who we really are; " I am an expression of the Divine impulse", I am light manifesting as a human body", etc. Eventually, as our desire to know ourselves expands, and our identification with the external reality shrinks, we become dis-illusion-ed with the world, our friends, our job, and ourselves. This is a good time to take some time away from it all, usually by going back to nature. The curious thing about nature is that it doesn't label itself. It doesn't strive to understand, to quantify and qualify. It doesn't ask questions. It just is! This is the next key to knowing yourself; just be and the rest will take care of itself. If you stop moving, and breathe, the most amazing truths will become self-evident. Spend a day being like a tree, and the cosmos will reveal itself. Sit by a stream, and the water will tell you all, as if the Divine itself were sitting next to you.

If you can stop your need to be someone long enough, the true you will begin to speak to you; of all that you are, EVERYTHING, of all that you know, EVERYTHING, and of all that you've been, EVERYTHING. This is the beginning of the Divine connection we all seek. Again, the Divine paradox is, that to make the connection, we must first decide not to seek anything, but instead to actively dis-associate ourselves with everything, so that the connection can come through. The Creator has been speaking all the time, but we have been unable to hear the message through all the static. Remove the static, and Bingo! someone's talking, and what's being said is totally true, totally resonant, and totally right on! In fact this voice is better at spelling it all out than any guide/guru/psychic we've ever given our power away to!

For those who seek the truth, the Divine is the ultimate source, and we all have a personal phone line that costs us nothing, that answers any question, and that knows us better than we know ourselves. All we need to do is decide to tune in; nothing to dial, no one to set up an account with, no possibility of ever being disconnected. No matter where we are, we can ask a question, and get an immediate response. As you do this you begin to see a much bigger picture, a larger frame of reality. You begin to see with the Divine's eyes, to know what the Divine knows. It all becomes clear, and you can forgive it all, and know it is all in the Creator's hands. You begin to see that you can have anything you want, just by asking, because that is the Divine grace. You never need to limit yourself to who someone else wants you to be. The Divine wants you to be who you really are, and so do you. After this becomes clear, and you re-member, and re-connect, you are ready to serve. And the only service there is, is to help everyone to be themselves by reconnecting to the Divine. Once the world is reconnected, and operating through Divine guidance, then we can all take a deep breath together, as one Divine being, and become whatever we all desire ourself to be. We are all expressions of the Divine, that is what we truly are!

THE WHOLE
IS STILL
NO MOVEMENT

NOTHING TO SEE
NO ONE TO SEE IT

NO FORM
AND
NO CONCEPTION OF
FORM

STASIS,STILLPOINT

LACK OF AWARENESS
LACK OF AWARENESS OF
AWARENESS

NO ONE DREAMING
AND NO ONE
AWAKE

NO DARKNESS, NO LIGHT

A PERFECT BALANCE
OF OPPOSITES
CANCELLING EACHOTHER
OUT
A PERFECT UNION OF
COMPETING FORCES
CREATING NOTHING

ABSOLUTE ABSENCE

SENSELESS, VOICELESS
TIMELESS, DESIRELESS
MOTIONLESS, FORMLESS

NOTHING TO COMMUNICATE
NO ONE TO COMMUNICATE TO

NO VOLITION
NO MEANING
NO URGE

PERFECT SYMMETRY
EVERYTHING IN ITS PLACE
AND ACCOUNTED FOR

NO NEED FOR PLACEMENT
NO NEED FOR DECISION
NO NEED FOR ACTION

NO OPINION, NO JUDGEMENT
NOTHING TO JUDGE

NO INTERACTION
NOTHING TO INTERACT

NOTHING TO SAY
NOTHING TO DO
NOWHERE TO GO

NO MEETING OF THE MINDS
NO MINDS TO MEET

DESCRIPTION IS NONEXISTENT
THEREFORE NO VOICE TO SPEAK
LANGUAGE IS UNDISCOVERED

CONTEMPLATION IS IMPOSSIBLE
MEDITATION IS USELESS
EVEN IF THERE WERE SOMEONE TO MEDITATE
THERE IS NOTHING TO MEDITATE UPON

NO LIGHT TO SEE BY
NO DARK TO PENETRATE
NO COLOR TO SET FORM APART
NO CONTRAST, NO DISTINCTION

NO VIBRATION
NOTHING TO VIBRATE

NO FEELING, OR TOUCH, OR SENSATION
NO EXPERIENCE OF ANYTHING AT ALL
WHATSOEVER
FOREVER: BLANK, VOID, EMPTY, UNFORMED
PERFECTLY BALANCED, NO TENSION, SILENT, STILL
BEREFT OF SENSATION, UNAWARE, COMPLETE, FINISHED
INDESCRIBABLE, CONSTANT, UNCHANGING

THIS IS GOD
THIS IS THE SOURCE
THIS IS WHERE WE BEGIN
AND WHERE WE END

INTERMISSION, INTERLUDE, TAKE A BREAK, THINK ABOUT IT, EXAMINE THE GREAT VOID

A FLICKER, AN URGE
AN INSPIRATION

SUDDEN, IMPERCEPTIBLE
YET UNDENIABLE

A PUSH, A PULL, A FLASH
A RIPPLE, SOUNDLESS AND UNSEEN
BUT UNFORGETTABLE

A BREATH, A SIGH
UNHEARD BY ANYONE, UNRECOGNIZED
BUT INDISPUTABLE

A DESIRE, A GLIMPSE
A SCENT ON THE BREEZE
NOTHING IS THERE BUT
FOR A MOMENT...

A SOUND OR A FEELING
TOO LOW TO HEAR
TOO SOFT TO SENSE
TOO BRIEF TO AKNOWLEDGE

THEN IT IS GONE, BUT
WHAT WAS IT?

A COLOR, A DISTINCTION, A CONTRAST
AN INSTANT OF TIME, A WORD, A THOUGHT
AN AWARENESS, A COMMUNICATION, AN IDEA
A NOISE, A TOUCH, A TICKLE, A KNOWING

NOBODY'S THERE TO KNOW IT
AND THEN IT IS GONE

SILENCE,
SILENCE,
SILENCE,
SILENCE

A FLICKER

SILENCE,
SILENCE,
SILENCE

A SOUND

SILENCE
SILENCE
A THOUGHT
SILENCE

A WORD, AN IDEA, AN AWARENESS, A DESIRE

SILENCE

A COLOR, A SCENT, A BREEZE, A TOUCH, A SMILE

SILENCE

A SHOUT, A FLASH, AN INSPIRATION, A DESIRE, A DANCE

SILENCE

A PURPOSE, A FRAMEWORK, A FORMING, A DREAM, A VISION
A SONG, A VIBRATION, A RIPPLE IN TIME

SILENCE

A SYMPHONY, A RHYTHM, A CONTINUUM, A MELODY,
A STORY, A MOVEMENT
A CACOPHONY OF SENSATION, A PLETHORA OF IDEAS,
A STREAMING OF DESIRE
AN OCEAN OF COMMUNICATION, A PANDEMONIOUM OF
INTERSECTING, UNRELATED
AWARENESSES, UNSTOPPABLE, UNDIRECTED, UNCONSCIOUS,
UNBALANCING THE SILENCE
BOWLING OVER THE STILLNESS, WRENCHING APART THE
PERFECTION, COMPETING FOR
ATTENTION, AND SPACE AND AWARENESS, RIPPING ACROSS THE
EMPTINESS, SPLITTING
UP THE UNION, DESTROYING THE NOTHINGNESS

THIS IS CHAOS
THIS IS CREATION
THIS IS MADNESS
THIS IS THE BEGINNING OF THE END
THIS IS GOD, AND
THIS IS US

THIS IS ALL THAT IS

AND AGAIN THERE IS

S I L E N C E...

A BREATH, A CONTEMPLATION, AN UNDERSTANDING, A BREAK IN THE MUSIC

AN INTERMISSION

WHAT HAVE WE DONE AND WHO ARE WE?

WHO ARE WE?

AWARENESS, DESIRE, THOUGHT, ACTION, VIBRATION, SOUND, LIGHT, COLOR, SENSATION,
TOUCH, FEELING, THE BREEZE, THE SUN, THE NIGHT, THE COLD, THE RIPPLES THROUGH
THE SILENCE, THE BALANCE, THE PERFECTION, THE SYMMETRY, THE ABSENCE, THE
CHAOS

WE ARE ALL THAT IS

WHAT HAVE WE DONE?

WE HAVE DISTURBED THE EQUILIBRIUM, WE HAVE INVADED THE TIMELESSNESS
WE HAVE SHATTERED THE SYMMETRY

WE HAVE EXPANDED ALL THAT IS

WE ARE THE GOD OF ETERNAL NOTHINGNESS
WE ARE THE GOD OF CONSTANT EVERYTHINGNESS

WHERE DO WE GO FROM HERE?

Let me tell you a story:

A long time ago, during the time of chaos, an "idea" was floating on the winds of awareness, with no particular place to go. This "idea" was very fluid, and was constantly changing itself according to various urges and desires it encountered while it floated. This "idea" had no conception of the notion of discrimination, which would become popular much later in the greater story that was unfolding, and so this "idea" just gathered urges and desires along its path, without concerning itself with where they fit in, in the greater scheme of things that was then unfolding, or, and this is central to our story, how they interacted with each other.

Now, somewhat later in the time of chaos, though at this stage the concept of time was still in its infancy, this "idea" became rather heavy in relation to the winds of awareness, which were still very light so as to get above it all and get perspective, and so it slowly descended from the upper reaches of the awareness stream, through the middle reaches, where resided many of the other ideas who were at that time rapidly expanding the concept of the middle path, and were later to be known as the "middling ideas", and eventually it found itself in the lower reaches of the awareness stream.

Now, once this "idea" landed at the bottom fringe, it noticed that it wasn't moving very fast, as a matter of fact it wasn't moving at all relative to the awareness stream, and this gave it a chance to look around, so to speak. It also noticed, and here we're being generous since noticing things wasn't this "idea's" strong suit, that there were no other ideas in the vicinity, at least none that were recognizable as such. As a matter of fact there wasn't anything at all in the vicinity. This "idea" was truly on its own.

Having found itself in a spot, ain't that the truth!, and not moving, and all alone, this "idea" began experiencing some very unusual sensations. These sensations were the result, and this would become very clear over time, of all the urges and desires this "idea" had accumulated fighting each other for this "idea's" attention. This fighting for attention was something that had been happening for quite some time, due to the limited space this "idea" had reserved for self-awareness when it began its journey. The space was so limited that this idea could only really attend one urge or desire at a time, forcing the others to be stacked up like firewood against the back wall until their turn came. So, the urges and desires, having been accumulated willy-nilly and stuffed into eachother, began to suffocate from lack of room to express, leading to the sensation this "idea" had of getting so nauseous that it felt it might just have to throw up! In fact “the urge to throw up” had managed to unite with “the desire to express fully”, and they had pushed their way into this "idea's" awareness, forcing it to come to grips with the situation .

And so, after turning various shades of purple, and making the most disgusting faces, this "idea" made a momentous decision, actually its first and only real decision, since accumulating every urge and desire that exists without discrimination can't be considered true decisiveness, and in a burst of sensation never experienced before or since, every last urge and desire in all of awareness flew from the bowels of this "idea" outward, madly expressing all the pent up, repressed, and denied aspirations they represented, and seriously undermining the rest of awareness' tranquility and order in the process!

Thus the Universe was born, and the rampant excesses of that latter period of chaos are well documented throughout eternity, and, I might add, still being felt in random moments of personal experience. But I get ahead of myself.

So, what became of this "idea", who was after all the architect of life as we know it? Did he just return to the awareness stream after relieving himself of his self-created stomach ache? Did he bask in the brilliance of the upper reaches of awareness never again to sully himself with the nitty-gritty of the lower dimensions? Well, oddly enough, no.

You see our"idea", and it really is all ours as you shall soon see, having once experienced the fullness of everything, and the emptiness of nothing, couldn't just turn around and return to the blissful contentment of nothingness, nor could it ride the waves of awareness, looking on as an uninvited spectator while time and the Universe hurtled towards its destiny. You see our"idea", in its moment of supreme release, found that it was not totally empty. It had released its burden of the sensations of awarenss, but it still was self-aware. Our "idea" had experienced creating the Universe, and through that act it had created something completely new, something it hadn't been aware of before, memory! As our "idea" floated, and remembered what had happened, it created, through memory, a record of its existence, an existence that, though it existed, was not aware that it existed, causing immense problems for all concerned, who weren't concerned yet because they weren't aware that they were concerned, etc., etc....The record of our "idea's" existence was contained in the slot formerly occupied by all the urges and desires, which were now roaming freely, in rampant expression, all over the Universe.

Now, since our "idea" had the ability to monitor only one thing at a time, it decided that this memory thing was just too cool to ignore, and so, and this is critical to our story, our "idea" spent every available minute remembering itself creating the Universe, over, and over, and over, and over again!

Meanwhile, back at the ever-expanding ranch of "all that is", "all that is" was reaching a turningpoint in its existence. After the "Big Ralph" occurred, all the urges and desires went spinning out, individually expressing their isness to the utmost of their ability. Eventually, each had reached a limit in the number of ways they could do this alone. They wanted something more, and this brings us to the big shift, from the end of the age of chaos, to something new, and something blue, and something true, etc. This was the age of relationships!

So, while our "idea" was busy contemplating its navel endlessly, to the exclusion of everything else, "all that is" decided, in a flash of inspiration, to put its heads, and everything else, together and get physical! You see, up until this point in time, the characters in our drama were all pretty tenuous in the physical department; actually they were physically nonexistent, but since no one was there to say so......, and therefore they had no sense of boundaries, having left the only home they knew when our "idea" lost its cookies. So, as they expressed themselves, they were constantly interacting with eachother, but it wouldn't amount to much, or to anything at all , a lot like some groups I know, but that is another story. So, like I said, they put their parts together, as best they could, and they decided to make something of themselves. At first they reached toward our "idea", in the hope that they could squeeze back in there, but, first off, they couldn't get its attention, memory being even then something a lot more interesting than the Universe. It turns out that "all that is" had expanded itself so much, through all that expressing it had done since the big splurf, that there wasn't even room for one urge in all its glory to fit into our "idea's" limited awareness receptacle. It was a lot like trying to put a newly hatched chic back into its mother chicken. They decided to give up.

Having been refused entry, by the original bolimic, the newly bonded actors in our cosmic drama found themselves extremely agitated, and frustrated, and at a loss as to what to do. Therefore, they did what all entities in their place would do. They proceeded to shout, and scream, and wave their arms, and run in circles all at once. As individual desires and urges this by itself wouldn't have amounted to anything, but in their newly created state of common interest their close proximity, and sudden action, created a fierce implosion of energy, followed by an extreme explosion of energy. As one urge bumped into another urge, which bumped into a desire, etc. on down the line, this caused a giant chain reaction, which anyone with a rudimentary knowledge of physics can see was a recipe for disaster. This resulted in the next phase of "all that is", the "Big Bomb". Thus was created the physical Universe, or "all that is 2", now playing in a dimension near you! Of course, and this is the really interesting thing, our "idea" just happened to be next door, reliving the memories of its glorious past, when BOOM!, there goes the neighborhood. The explosion created a gazillion "mini-ideas", a gazillion "mini-urges", and a gazillion "mini-desires" rocketing all over the place.

Needless to say, our "idea" hadn't a clue as to what hit it, and neither did anyone else, but such is life in the fast lane; which is where everything was, hurtling out from the center at gazillions of parsecs per nanosecond. Before anyone could blink, and say WHUH?, all the "miniideas", "mini-urges', and "mini-desires" were stuck together in an infinite array of combinations, and found themselves in form, alive, in motion, and unable to do a thing about it.

Meanwhile, in the upper reaches of the awareness stream, things were cruising along just fine thank you; nothing to do, nowhere to go, no one to be, etc.. The events down below having happened in their own way, and in their own time; time and timelessness being tough to mix, a lot like oil and water, and what would be the point anyway?, the awareness stratosphere was patently oblivious that anything had happened, since nothing ever did!

The middling realms, however, were experiencing some pretty heavy weather, which is a pain in the butt when you're trying to stay on an even keel. All the middling ideas found themselves having a tough time discriminating, judging, placing, pigeonholing, removing, replacing, and just generally controlling all the new input they were receiving from below. It was a tough balancing act to stay aware, in control, on the path, and not stray off and get diverted by some lovely combination of urge/idea, or a really interesting desire/urge, or how about a truly magnificent desire/urge/idea? It was all just a bit too much, and many of the middling persuasion decided things would be so much better, and a damn sight easier, if everything reverted back to normal. The only problem was remembering what normal had been like. You see this memory stuff, invented by our "idea", or don't you remember?, could be very difficult. As more input, and experience, came in, you had to categorize it, make room for it, prioritize it, associate it, and a million other things. If you didn't it would just be a jumbled mess!

Anyway, needless to say, no one had a clue as to how it really had been before, though everyone knew it had been different. Going back to normal was just plain impossible, since the whole of "all that is" was going forward at horrendous speeds. Oh, attempts were made, you can be sure, to "stop this nonsense", and "behave", but it was all in vain, and if one middling idea took control for a moment, and all seemed headed for normalcy, soon enough a burst of active combining would occur somewhere in the "all that is", and before long the middling ideas would have to go back to the drawing board.

Many times over before the concept of conservation of matter was expressed, and even after, the middling crowd would try to wipe the slate clean and start over. "If you can't control them, then wipe them" was a supreme middling idea. Unfortunately for the middle, those urges and desires would just come back and, surprise, surprise, and this really floored the middling bunch, they would return really full of piss and vinegar, and often in ingenious forms that were very hard to pigeonhole, let alone control. And so there went another middling idea onto the compost pile of "all that is".

Now, as for the "upper crust awarenessians", the " nothing done, nothing done " crowd, all this rumble from the trenches, all this interstream squabbling, was much ado about nothing, which seemed kind of pointless, and all in all was disturbing what equilibrium remained in the "all that is". Peace, serenity, harmony, balance, tranquility, silence, the beyond, the beyond, this was the true way, at least for disembodied selfaware souls above the fray, and the sooner the physical end realized this the better for all concerned. So, the uppers and middles formed an alliance; each having their own agenda, but deciding that each couldn't accomplish anything alone; and they hit upon a plan of action, or nonaction for the uppers, who couldn't be bothered to act and so elected to observe. The middles would descend below just long enough to influence a selected group of lowers, those who were predisposed toward the "nowhere, nothing, no one" frame of mind. These lowers would be inspired, or threatened as the case may be and it often was, into inspiring others, through threats, to follow the true way. This inspiring/threatening was accompanied by various middling forms of violence, to impress those not yet inspired to get with the program, a course as we explained above that was doomed to failure, and if anything increased the problem!

The middlings had a modicum of success, but mostly with those that were non-doers anyway, and many setbacks, including more than a few middles who got very caught up in the drama of the unfolding "all that is", and refused to return to the middle way.

Meanwhile, back at awareness station "above it all", the nowhere beings observed it all with detatched nonschalance, mumbling sweet nothings under their breath like, "patience has its rewards", and "all things return to their source". But deep inside not a few of these "Gods", was a growing sense of doubt, and a continual feeling of uncertainty that they truly had the grand scheme of things wired. A council of the uppers was called at this point, and at it a younger, more idealistic, less selfimportant upper offered a new plan of action, a plan so ingenious that not one elder even said boo until he was done explaining it. This young upper would bypass the middling-meddlers, and go directly to the lowers himself, even going so far as to be born, horror of horrors, as a lower, and to grow up among them. At a certain point he would reveal himself, having gained their trust since he was one of them, and he would proceed to lay out the true way to them all. It was ingenious, it was sneaky, it was brilliant, and it was doomed to failure, but who wants to stop an ingenious young upper in full idealistic stride, especially in the land of "do not unto others"?

So, off went the youngster to give it the old college try, and try he did causing a whole lot of ancillary violence in the process, and his effort is remembered, though not in a completely uniform way, by millions of lowers who never even met the guy. In a real ironic twist the middles adopted his memory to further their own agenda, and succeeded more spectacularly using his story than with anything they had tried before.

Which brings us to the question at hand, namely: Where do we go from here?

Let us look at our cast of characters first:

"Uppers" Nothing to do, Nowhere to go, No one to be.

"Middles" Control all urges and desires, Walk the middle path, and if all else fails, " Try and wipe them out! "

"Lowers" Stuck in bodies that are made of urges and desires, trying to find the sanity in an insane "all that is", dealing with the vestiges of middling violence and Upper and Middle meddling, and subject to being wiped out if they don't get it right.

Now. who would you like to be?

Upper is simple, and streamlined, and very unrealistic in an everexpanding "all that is".

Middle is disciplined, and orderly, or violent, but close to impossible to achieve.

Lower is... well we all know lower don't we?

Now let's return to our prologue and summarize:

Step One: Nothing to see, or hear, or feel etc. No one to see it, hear it, feel it etc. The emptiness of eternity.

Step Two: A flicker, an urge, an inspiration etc., leading to chaos.

Step Three: A massive explosion leading to the physical version of "all that is. "

Conclusion:

Can it be that all that we are, is nothing, and everything, at the same time/untime? If we were nothing once, we can be nothing again. If we are "all that is", then we can be "all that is", and nothing, since nothing + "all that is" = "all that is" !

The **uppers** choose step one; but having chosen something, they automatically become part of the "all that is".

The **middles** want "nothing" more than anything, but by trying to wipe out something, namely the lowers, to get "nothing", they remove themselves from the middle path, and become part of the " all that is ".

And as for the **lowers** .... well we all know lowers, don't we?

BACK TO THE DRAWING BOARD!

How About:

Start with an idea, mix in various unstable elements, fuse them in a cosmic reaction, and Bingo!, Let's Party! Obviously the only course of action is to put our heads, and everything else, together, and go for the "**Big C02**" , that is:" **Cosmic Orgasm/Organism Squared** ", or the "**Little C02**", that is: "**Carbon Oxygen**" **TIMES "the Duality"**.

Since "the Duality" = "Everything/Nothing", WE ARE THE "BIG C02", AND WE ARE THE "SMALL C02".

So, if we form a critical mass, and realize our nothingness, and our"all that isness", accept our " Duality ", and go for the " Big C02 ", man we're in for the ride of our lives!

And won't we shake up that old awareness stream by hanging ten in the expanding " all that is " !!?!!

I say this is the only way to fly!

SO, FOR ALL YOU DO, AND DON'T DO, HERE'S LOOKING AT YOU, AND NOT YOU, NOW LET'S

CO2!

WISDOM COMES
IN SMALL DOSES
AND ONCE IT ARRIVES
MUST BE ASSIMILATED
ACCORDING TO
INDIVIDUAL BIAS AND
OPINION

THIS OFTEN LEADS
TO AN IMPERFECT UNDERSTANDING
BEING CODIFIED IN MEMORY
A MEMORY WHICH MUST BE DISCARDED
LATER ON
AS NEW INFORMATION
IS RECEIVED
THAT CONTRADICTS THE CODE
OF THE PAST

OLD INFORMATION:

WE ARE SEPARATE
WE ARE ALONE
WE ARE PURELY PHYSICAL BEINGS
WE ARE BEHOLDEN TO A GOD
WE DON'T CREATE OURSELVES
WE CAN'T CHANGE ANYTHING
WE MUST STRUGGLE AND KILL TO SURVIVE
WE MUST DIE SOMETIME
WE CAN NEVER TRUST ANYONE
WE CAN NEVER REALLY UNDERSTAND ANYTHING
WE MUST GIVE OUR POWER AWAY TO SURVIVE
WE MUST WORK FOR A LIVING
WE ARE TRAPPED BY OUR KARMA
WE CANNOT LEAVE THE EARTH PLANE BY OURSELVES
WE ARE ALL ALONE IN THE UNIVERSE

NEW INFORMATION:

WE ARE ONE
WE CREATE OURSELVES AND OUR ENVIRONMENT
WE CAN CHANGE EVERYTHING
WE KNOW IT ALL
WE ARE GOD
WE ARE ALL POWERFUL
WE CAN DO WHAT WE WANT
THERE IS NO KARMA
WE CAN LEAVE ANYTIME
WE NEVER DIE
WE ARE NEVER ALONE

Death is the flip-side of life, and they cancel eachother out freeing the soul to just be. Each having been experienced we can choose either at any time, or we can choose neither, which is the same as choosing both simultaneously. This is the cosmic paradox responsible for creation in the first place. We have been told that life is precious, but if that is so, then death must also be precious, since life and death are the same. If death is precious then we are required to consecrate it, which is the same as fully embracing it. Only be doing so, will we be able to grasp the new information, and restart creation as if nothing had ever happened before.

To die fully, we must first release all those souls who did not die fully and are polluting our environment with old information to make them feel better about their actions. Once we release these souls, we must release any and every idea, belief, or understanding we thought we had about anything and everything. We must release any connection we have with our environment as we perceive it now. If we can come to a place of seeing nothing, sensing nothing, thinking nothing, being nothing, and especially desiring and dreaming nothing, we will be able to die fully and assimilate the new information, creating a new beginning in the process.

We must dis-identify, un-describe, non-sense, and as this occurs resist the urge to replace the old with anything new. No new concepts, thoughts, ideas, pictures, feelings, understandings, desires, dreams, activities, NOTHING! New information will not be able to come into being until all the old information is gone and nothing has replaced it. Having done this, it will be possible to die fully, and begin anew the creation as if nothing ever happened, which is the truth! As the final remnants of something are released, and nothing takes their place, there will be a period of non-being that occurs. The old and the new are not compatible at all! The new must wait until the old dissappears completely so that the new beginning may fully happen here on the Earth.

The End
of
the Age

This is the end of one age, and the beginning of another. What this means is that one age is winding down, and another is winding up, and they are meeting eachother on the big highway of the Universe. Old agers are crossing paths with new agers, and this makes for some pretty interesting scenarios throughout the world. It's almost like a cosmic musical chairs, with everyone scrambling as the old age dies and the new wave arrives from the source celestial. The old agers can sense the shift, even if its only unconsciously, and they're trying to get with the beat, but their programming gets in the way. If these oldies hang with the newies too long, it begins to push all their buttons, and they begin to preach oldie philosophy left and right. The newies just shrug and figure, "let them rant, they haven't got a whole lot of time left anyway".

All that it takes for the old agers to cop a new age chair is an open mind. You see the big joke is: in this musical chairs there's enough room for everyone; if you can release your programming, and groove to the new reality. This is tough slogging for oldies with constant broadcasts in their heads, but some are trying hard and scoring points with the celestial rating agents. Let's face it, some of the advance guard of the new age have got their share of faulty input to clear, and it ain't so easy ! It takes alot of listening and breathing. Sometimes you begin to feel that dying might be a whole lot easier than facing the music and riding the big wave!

In the new age alot of things are going to be different. I mean, probably no monday night football, maybe no television at all, and probably not any coffee! So, lots of us are getting our last licks in while we can. It's like a new year's party, where you say goodbye to last year, while you enjoy every last bit of it while you can. Once it's over how many of us spend any time thinking about it? Not many!

Once the new age arrives, and we party out the old, there's no looking back. So right now we are nostalgic, as we sense the shifting of the seasons from winter to spring, and we begin to see green shoots springing up everywhere. There still might be a late frost, or two, but soon enough here comes the sun, the warmth, the sweet smells of a new birth all around us. Any day now summer will be upon us.

So, get your kicks, remember how it all was, all of it, while you can. Reminisce with the oldies, and the newies, relive those past lives, watch t.v., drive your car like there's no tomorrow, get mad at those stupid politicians, crooks, and C.I.A. assholes, even pay your taxes while you still can! And then, one day, it'll all be gone. You'll look around you, and everything will be brand new. Not even a vestige of the past to remind you. Even the inner landscape of your being will be swept clean. It's all being washed away to make room for the new.

This crossing of the ages will contain it's own fair share of chaos to be sure. Some of this is spelled out in the bible, and in new age publications. Suffice to say major Earth-shifts are in order, so hold on to your hat! Here are some handy-dandy predictions for the curious part of you that wants to know what's around that corner:

In 1992 volcanic activity will really start to take off, as madre Earth begins to release some of that inner tension she's been holding in for so long. The Phillipines and Japan are right over a major tension spot, and what we've seen so far is just a little deep breathing to get the energy moving. Europe's release should be coming up pronto, as will Alaska, and the Pacific Northwest. Mount St. Helens was just a friendly warning from our mother that she's serious about releasing her emotions. So watch out Mt. Ranier, and Mt. Hood fans! Mt. Shasta new agers shouldn't put all their hard earned cash on land just yet either.

As for the Soviet Union, it's gonna be a tough 1992 Earth-shifting wise, so stay on your toes and keep breathing. This is your big lesson in nonattatchment as many, many old agers say goodbye to the planet. Let them go with love in your heart, it's their choice, and theirs alone.

1992 is the year that China has been waiting for. Tienanmen's chickens are coming home to roost, and the oldest place on Earth is about to get it's butt kicked. This is the wake up call for the old men, and the rest of the one billion plus, in the land of the ancients. Earthquakes, floods, volcanoes, tidal waves, hail, sudden freezes, boiling heat, plagues, China will see it all from 1992-1996, as nature's wrath is released throughout Asia. It will be a great cleansing, and purification, of the stagnation that has festered there despite the Mother's constant urging to release and open.

Central and South America are also ripe for a shift. The winter of 1991-1992 should see some major volcanic activity. The recent cholera epidemic is just for openers on the disease front. Look for new plagues to start in South America winter of 1991-1992, and begin to move north. The U.S. is very vulnerable to the spreading of these disesase waves, and they will not stop at our border no matter what the experts say. The kundalini of the Earth should awaken sometime in January - March 1992, throughout Central America, as the old energy in the pyramids is cleansed and the new energy comes in. A great shaking will occur all along the land from Mexico to Panama, and into South America. There may be a major land break along this stretch as Southern and Northern hemispheres of the Earth move in different directions.

Africa will be relatively free of volcanic activity except in the very North and very South. However, the whole continent will be swept by famine and disease of such epic proportions that by 1996 much of Africa will be a total wasteland.

Greenland will warm up and begin to melt in late 1992, as will Antarctica. Iceland will be completely overrun with magma and will have to be evacuated.

The east coast of North America will experience the "Big One" from Canada to the Carolinas, and many, many will die. This quake may occur early in 1992 or later in 1993, depending on the shifts elsewhere. The whole of the Carribbean basin will be swept by massive storms in 1992, and the Atlantic ridge will erupt bringing Atlantis up from the deep from Florida to the Azores. This "ridge raising" will probably occur after 1993, depending again on what occurs before, and what consciousness shifts humankind makes as well.

Australia and New Zealand will be relatively unaffected by Earth-shaking types of activity, but I foresee some kind of major environmental disaster there in late 1991, or early 1992 that will have lasting effects on their rich fishing grounds. This will also cause those two countries to become even more isolationist than they are now.

By mid-1994, the whole world will be in major environmental upheaval, and mass migrations may occur as whole regions become uninhabitable. This will have various effects on world politics. Some areas, like Europe, may attempt to become police states to control immigration. This probably won't succeed very well. Other regions may join forces to help dispel mass hysteria and riot. The most devastating effect will be on the food sources of the world. The U.S. heartland will be hit by drought and flood in 1992, wiping out any excess production for world markets. Europe may not be able to feed itself, once seismic activity really takes off, and this will be disastrous for the region. Russia will be o.k. in many areas, but distribution to the cities will possibly halt completely causing a mass exodus back to the farm. By 1994 Russia will truly earn its label as a peasant society. Other parts of the Soviet Union will be in trouble, and there will bee extreme turmoil and mass movements of people. China will be completely unable to feed its huge population, and civil war will break out as people fight for whatever they can find to eat.

Japan will be in a very bad way with no way to import food, and the wealthiest will attempt to buy their way into America, Australia, and New Zealand. Subsistence farming countries like Guatemala and Peru may be o.k. foodwise, but other troubles will cause mass death and relocation. The Middle East will be in the biggest fix of all. The West's disrupted economies will not be able to import oil, nor will they have any extra food to export. Ironically, the country in the best position to feed itself is Iraq, which occupies the fertile crescent, the biblical "Garden of Eden". If Iraq transfers its penchant for arms to farming it will be able to export food to its neighbors. If not, there could be a war in the region as countries like Saudi Arabia, with no arable land, seek to gain some with force. The advent of the Anti-Christ on the world stage, in late 1996 or early 1997, will forestall the wholesale slaughter of Armageddon, for a while, but it still could get ugly in a hurry.

For the U.S. the big worry is erratic weather causing bad harvest, massive disruption of the Eastern industrial regions, the importation of various plagues from the South, and perhaps the biggest bomb waiting to drop, Mexican refugees flooding in as things get worse and worse down South. Look for the U.S. to turn isolationist, and if things get too bad America will go to martial law, patrol its borders, and severely curtail dissent and unauthorized citizen activity. With a heavily armed population the cities of America could become major battlegrounds. The best place to be will be high in the mountains away from the action. Selfsufficient agriculture and animal husbandry would be good things to practice in case the worst becomes a reality. As always, a strong connection to Spirit will be your best course of action when the going gets rough. Remember, what we're seeing is the ushering out of the old age and the welcoming in of the new. There is only room at the inn for one age, and the old is getting the boot. So be glad, sing praises to this cosmic exchange, wave goodbye to the old, and get ready for the new reality coming to a dimension near you. Stay attuned!

Vision

Vision is the ability to move beyond your current circumstances and see a possible future that lies ahead. Each moment we are alive an infinite array of possible futures spreads out from wherever we are in the moment. It is up to us, through the medium of choice, to grasp any of these futures and make it happen. First of all, however, we must become aware of the possible avenues open to us. To do this we use our capability for invision-ing what might lie ahead. Then we ask for guidance to show us what each future might entail for us. We expand ourselves beyond the present and sweep the horizon with our inner eye, asking Spirit to provide answers to any questions we may have concerning each avenue we seek.

Part of the visioning process for us entails the setting of goals. What is it we would really like to see in our life? These goals give us and Spirit something to found our vision upon. Do we want certain material forms in our life? Or, do we have spiritual aspirations? These goals are very helpful when we are trying to manifest our vision in a concrete, and physical, way. One of the realities of being in a body is that most of our visions have a practical component. We seek to meet our physical needs so that spiritual awakening will be easier.

Many of the world's spiritual teachers have taught that the physical necessities get in the way of true spiritual awareness. Many of us are questioning this reasoning right now, however, and a new group has arisen in the new age community, the "Spiritual Materialists". They say that you can have whatever you want in this life, be as comfortable as possible, then open yourself up to spiritual teachings and experiences. To discuss the validity of this we must return to the visioning process.

Remember, we said that part of the process involves choice. You sit in the moment, in-vision your future possibilities, seek guidance from Spirit, and then choose a future to go for. Each choice must, of necessity, have risks as well as rewards attatched to it. Some of these we can see, and others are hidden. Even with Spirit's guidance, we can never know all that a given future holds. The Creator likes to keep us guessing a lot, and this is often how we learn, through our reactions and adaptations to surprise conditions that arise.

Now, we were saying that the "Spiritual Materialists" seek all the comfort that they can get, in a practical physical way, before they seek spiritual awakening. Their future choices must therefore entail manifesting these comforts, they seek guidance from Spirit to see these futures' consequences before they make a choice. Each choice you make shifts your present position, and opens new futures to your vision. However, a natural law that applies to this process states: " energy flows where attention goes". The array of possible futures, though infinite in the truest sense, actually follows this law in a practical way. As you make one choice the futures shift in a parallel manner, as Spirit senses your personal attunement and provides you with what you seek. For the "Spiritual Materialists" this means that their vision process opens up all kinds of avenues for material comfort, and this framework continues to build new futures around this central focus. Of course around the periphery they may be sensing other possibilities, but in the center, glowing brightly, is their prime tenet; get comfortable!

If we return to our visioning process, we will see what could shift this focus and bring a new focus into the future. As we sit in our moment, we vision our futures, and we ask for guidance. Aha!, here is a key. We can at this point ask Spirit to show us another way to go. This gives Spirit the leeway to become creative with our infinite array of futures. But, if we continue in the same vein for quite awhile, our choices have so much momentum, and it is almost impossible for us to change our ways. We return to what we know, to what is comfortable. We don't take risks, and true spiritual awakening entails enormous risks. So what do we do? We're in a rut and we know it, but we can't seem to change. The key here is choice, not our own choice but Spirit's choice. If we are to shift our focus, we must release our need to be right, to be in control, to be in charge, to know it all. Just once we must say, "Spirit, I'm in a rut, I don't know anything, help me out here, you make the choice". This is a momentous step for ego-centered beings to take, and often they must experience a lot of pain to make this shift. Once you make it, however, your life is never the same again.

So, when you vision your future, don't set conditions, don't limit your options, instead become unlimited. Say, "Spirit, you can see it all, you decide what's best for me; best in terms of my true path, best in terms of my desire to learn, to grow, and evolve ". This is what vision is really about. Not just replacing today's tired reality with something the same, but really opening the way to new, unlimited realities. This is what we all truly seek in our lives, and why we all feel a little empty, even if we're comfortable. Since energy follows attention, the sky's the limit. So go for it! In-vision with Spirit's all-seeing eyes, and believe me you'll be pleasantly surprised.

The Origin of the Chakras

A lot of attention has been paid, in the new age, to the chakras. What exactly are these wheels of light, and what do they do for us?

The human body is essentially a liquid crystal transformer that steps down the powerful electrical impulses pulsing out from the source of all things. This ability to step down energy is necessary to create this illusionary world we call physical reality. Light must be slowed down dramatically for it to appear in physical form; to be solid to our eyes and our sense of touch. For anything to appear in the physical realms, it must transform the light of truth into the form of illusion.

In the beginning times, as beings of light, we desired to create a playground for ourselves, and we used our ability to shift form at will to change ourselves around as we played. This, however, did not give us a permanent place to play in, just an infinite array of roles to play. Eventually, with the Creator's help, we learned to step down the energies of pure light, by prisming it through our own energy field. This broke the true light up into seven distinct color bands or spectrums. By combining these we created the physical Universe of frozen light that we live in now. Thus we created our playground to create in, and we prismed the light into all the various forms we could ever imagine. We then named these forms, and experimented by sending our own energy into the forms to see what it would be like to exist as form. In this way we began to know creation, and eachother, intimately through our interactions in our different disguises. This was the time on Earth known as Pangea; we were all together and the Earth was one large land mass.

Now, as with anything, some of us enjoyed the playground more than the others, and those souls began to spend more and more time in forms, and less time as creatures of light. As they did this the forms began to become more and more solid, more frozen, more transformed. Before this everything that was created was essentially a rainbow of light in a particular shape. These contained every color that makes up the true light, and these colors shimmered up and down creating the illusion of form. As the players of the game got more into the game their personal energy began to manipulate these forms from within, and their rainbow energy would interact with a form's energy making it appear much more solid. Eventually, some of these players decided to stay in a particular form for longer and longer periods, interacting with other players who did the same. These players became lost in the illusion, and refused to acknowledge any of us who were outsde of form at all! This was the beginning of the time on the Earth known as Lemuria.

As these forms became more and more solid, and the players became more and more a part of the illusion, some of the forms were purposely altered to contain only a part of the whole rainbow spectrum. This caused them to be less changeable in form. Thus the players could predict the form their playground would take as they played their games. Another function of this more extreme stepdown and transformation, was the the beginning of the concept of distinction on the Earth. Before this, since everything was a rainbow, there was no true distinction because the forms were constantly changing. Now it was possible to distinguish the single or multi-color form from the rainbow surroundings, and one's own form from the other player's form.

Gradually the players, instead of inventing new forms to play with from the rainbows, began to manipulate the more solid forms, combining them together and creating new forms. These players began to distinguish themselves from those who were more changeable, and who played with the rainbow forms. The more frozen group moved away from the rainbows and began to create massive forms of frozen light. They also occupied bodies that were frozen and which contained only part of the true light. This was the beginning of the period of Earth time known as Atlantis.

The Atlanteans began to distinguish themselves more and more as their society grew, and as they did so they gradually found it more and more difficult to shift into and out of the different forms they created. Some of them became very alarmed at this inability to leave form. The Lemurians, who played with the rainbow forms, were still able to move into and out of form at will. The Atlanteans that were trapped in form began to become more and more anxious as they tried to leave and couldn't. This anxiety registered in their forms, darkening them and blocking out more of the true light that poured forth continuously from the Creator. These blockages restricted some of the free movement the players had started out with, and this caused them even more anxiety. To compensate for this lack of movement, the blocked ones began to manipulate their environment to substitute for their deficiencies. This brought the Atlantean civilization to a very high level of technology in a relatively short period of time. Unfortunately, the technology didn't compensate for the paranoia that occurred in those trapped in form. At this time some of the Lemurians began to interact with the Atlanteans, and they tried to help them to leave their bodies. Some were helped to leave for a short time, but their fear brought them back in. This caused even more fear. Toward the end of this time many of the Atlanteans began to feel powerless and hopeless, and they overcompensated for this by enslaving the Lemurians that were visiting, and doing horrible experiments on them in the guise of trying to fix the problems the Atlanteans had created through their own ignorance in the first place. Just before Atlantis destroyed itself, by overamping the great crystal it used to power its technology, some of these experimenters managed to create a new body form, and they trapped a number of Lemurians in it. When the big crystal blew, and caused the Earth to shift on its axis, almost the whole Atlantean civilization was destroyed except for a small group, including some of these scientists who took these body forms into their ships and escaped. This remnant continued their experiments in space, and when they returned to land they released all these body forms, except for one group which was very dark. This dark group was enslaved and used as labor to try and recreate Atlantis. All the other forms, with trapped Lemurians in them, became the root races that repopulated the world after the shift.

These embodied Lemurians were still fully connected to the true light source, they just couldn't manage to leave the forms they were trapped in. The rainbow world of Lemuria was unaffected by the shift, but the trapped ones couldn't really interact with it in their limited body forms. The rainbow Lemurians still continued to play in their rainbow world, shifting in and out, creating and recreating their world constantly. After the Earthshift, the trapped Lemurians looked at their world, and themselves, and saw that both were very solid in appearance. They also noticed that the rainbow colors, that had constantly shimmered in Lemuria, seemed to have frozen in place in their bodies. The colors had become separate balls of color that spun in place, but they didn't seem to interact with eachother like in Lemuria. Each race of trapped Lemurians had bodies that took on the color of whatever ball of light was most dominant. There were seven root races total: Red, Orange, Yellow, Green, Blue, Indigo, and Violet. Each individual had seven balls of light in his body, and these are the modern chakras we know today. The Atlanteans had white bodies, but they had become disconnected from the true light, and their bodies were also made up of the seven chakras.

The seven root races were aware that the Atlanteans were trying to recreate Atlantis, and they desired to create a civilization of their own. Thus began a great creative endeavor, as all the root races worked together to create, what was known in the bible as the Tower of Babel. Each of the root races found they had a unique power that the other races lacked, and so each began to specialize in what they did best. The Red race was very good at powerful, energetic work. The Orange could move things using energy extended from their lower bodies. The Yellow used their willpower to create things. The Green used energy in the middle of their bodies to enliven their creations. The Blue used soundwaves to bring things into form. The Indigo used their inner-eye to vision what they wanted to create into form. The Purple could bring a very powerful light from the top of their heads to create with. Each of these energies is concentrated in the particular chakra points we have today. The root races were psychically attuned to eachother, through their common Lemurian heritage, and they accomplished amazing things together after the shift. The Tower of Babel was actually a civilization very close to the sophistication of the original Atlantis, and it was obvious to the remnant Atlanteans that if it continued it would become the dominant force on the Earth. These remnants, being fear oriented beings, and having unconscious guilt about the experiments they had done to the Lemurians, thought that the Lemurian root races would seek to enslave or destroy them once they became all-powerful. Therefore, in a preemptive strike, the remnant Atlanteans attacked the Tower of Babel and destroyed it. In the ensuing confusion they separated each root race, and placed each on a separate land mass, so they couldn't continue to cooperate together. From then on the Atlanteans kept an eagle eye on each race, and they implanted the subtle idea that each race was somehow superior to the others, and that it must prove its superiority by wiping out the other races when they came in contact. The Atlanteans set themselves up as God, and sent each race against the others in constant warfare, so that they would never again get together and become the dominant force on the planet.

Unknown to the remnant Atlanteans, another group of Atlanteans, ones that had tried to stop the forces that eventually destroyed Atlantis, had escaped the destruction as well. This group had gathered a record of all that had occurred since the beginning times, and secreted it out of harm's way. These Atlanteans realized that the only way out of the morass the fearful ones had created was to bring this true record to the root races, and train them to realign their rainbow energy with the Creator's true light so that they could leave their bodies once again. After the dispersal of the root races these Atlanteans, later to be known as the White Brotherhood, sent emissaries to each race, and began to train volunteers in the realignment process. Thus began the classic struggle on the Earth between the forces of light and the forces of darkness; a struggle that is playing itself out to a final conclusion in the time we find ourselves living in right now!

Many of us have spent time on the Earth as emissaries of the White Brotherhood, and we have returned at this time to tell our stories, and to help others to remember who they really are. We know that we are truly all one being, and that we are all rainbow lightbeings, extensions of the true light of the Creator. We are not interested in constant warfare to prove our superiority, and we are re- remembering how to use our inner rainbows to create an outer rainbow world of peace, creativity, and truth. We are creating, in the physical world, a counterpart to the rainbow lightworld of Lemuria that has always been present just beyond the vision of the physical senses. Many of us are contacting this rainbow lightworld consciously, and communicating with our brothers and sisters in Lemuria. This is our future; to bring the lightworld and physical world together, to bring the Heaven we all came from to Earth, and to heal the old wounds inflicted upon us by paranoid, trapped, Atlantean souls who were afraid of what they themselves had created. We are here to teach these beings that we are all one, and that we can all live together without fear. Together we can create a rainbow world of the true light in physical form. One day soon our inner world of shimmering rainbows will merge with our outer world, and we will all be one big spinning ball of infinite rainbow light!

Dis-Ease
and
Modern Medicine

Modern medicine at this time is attempting to overpower disease through brute force. Unfortunately, this is a method that tends to fail in its ability to heal. The eradication of disease, through cutting it out, irradiating it, or trying to kill it with chemicals, for example, only leads to major trauma for the patient, his body, his psyche, his nervous system, etc. This war against disease changes none of the causes of the disease itself.

Dis-ease aptly describes the condition of someone who is not at-ease with himself, his world, his life path etc. Why would someone not be at ease? The causes could be infinite in scope and possibility. This is part of the reason that uniform cures by modern medicine are not effective in the long run.

In terms of natural law, the body or physical dimension of the individual soul is the final stage of the energy chain. It is a step down in energy from the spiritual, mental and emotional levels of reality. Therefore, any dis-ease must first begin somewhere in these higher vibrational levels, and then move down until it contacts the physical body. By the time someone experiences a physical manifestation of dis-ease, they have been experiencing one or more of these higher level manifestations for quite some time. Unfortunately, many souls these days are not consciously aware of any of these realms in a personal way, and that includes the physical! People just don't have time to be aware of their thoughts, feelings, inner guidance, or that pain in their chest until it is so debilitating that they can't block it out any longer. Thus it is very easy for a full blown, possibly terminal dis-ease to develop seemingly out of thin air. Of course, if it gets to this point, and it is labeled terminal by modern medicine, people are subjected to the most ridiculous, useless, horrifying therapies which make them suffer even more and do absolutely nothing to help them become aware of the cause of their disease !

Dis-ease is the way Spirit guides us to stay on the path we chose before we incarnated onto the planet. When we were simply Spirit beings, these messages were received directly into our consciousness, and we acted accordingly. Now that we have taken on all kinds of dense levels of beingness, we are living on a multitude of levels simultaneously, and we must make a conscious effort to listen for guidance if we are to stay on our destiny path. If we don't decide to consciously attend to our guide, then Spirit must find other ways to get our attention. For the denser, more unconscious of us, this often means Spirit must really shout loud to break through all the internal static generated by all the conflicting selves fighting it out inside. Often, when Spirit comes in loud and clear, the message is completely ignored anyway because it conflicts with the ego-desire of the moment. This conflict is exactly what dis-ease really is; the dissonance between who we really are, and what we really came here to accomplish, and what the ego-self has enticed us to believe and do. Now that we are in a time of great transition on the planet, many of us need to wake up to our true self and get with whatever program we chose before we came in. If we are really dense, and we ignore the inner messages too long, Spirit will send us a little jolt of physical dis-ease to get our undivided attention. Remember, a lot of born-again Christians speak of some serious illness that caused them to seek spiritual help. When they were cured they had a shift in consciousness, and they sure spend an inordinate amount of time listening to the voice of Jesus in their ear now!

So, back to modern medicine. The A.M.A. crowd believes that we are all just a body, and that the body is just a machine that breaks down. They never seem to look for the cause of that breakdown, and thus many of their patients are cured of one dis-ease only to become ill later with another one, and another one, ad infinitum. This does wonders for the doctor's checkbook, but it isn't so great for the patient. Look at that word "patient". Does that ring any bells in your ear? If we want to attune ourselves to Spirit's guidance, and become Spirit-directed, we must practice a little patience. With a little patience comes a little trust and a little faith. With a little faith you can move mountains, so it should do wonders for your health! The most important thing about any dis-ease is the opportunity it gives us to look at our stuff, and to pay a little attention to our inner guidance. I've noticed that a fair amount of people are coming out of comas these days, and my intuitive sense is that while they were in there they paid some close attention to Spirit. They certainly act pretty different when they come out!

Now I am not saying that miracles can't happen with modern medicine, they can. Now that there are a large percentage of lightworkers present in the medical establishment, many more miracles are happening on a daily basis. Many doctors have become disillusioned with the politics of medicine, and have decided to open their hearts and minds in order to actually help people heal themselves. This is a major breakthrough, and things from now on will shift pretty fast. As the individual consciousness is expanded the structural realities will shift as well.

Each individual is ultimately responsible for their own healing process, and they will seek out help in direct proportion to their desire to heal. If what they really want is just a lot of attention, and people feeling sorry for them, the process could be a long one. Pretty soon here, if things are put off, they are going to have to find another planet to do their healing on! But that is their choice, and the show must go on. More and more souls are ready to heal now, to become Spirit-centered, and to act on their inner-guidance to begin to actualize their true life path. Many new techniques are being brought to the planet now to accelerate this process. During the transition ahead we will witness a multitude of spontaneous, miraculous cures. Most souls are at least unconsciously aware of the times we live in, and they are choosing to shift or leave the planet. Modern medicine has choices as well; to work with Spirit to guide people in their healing process, or gradually become obsolete in the new renaissance of medicine that is arriving on the planet. In the end it is the healing that is important, and we are all moving towards a healthy, at-ease, Spirit-directed, on- the- path planet. With Spirit's help we will all be at-ease very soon.

Feminine Energy

Feminine energy is becoming powerful on the Earth at this time. This is the receptive, intuitive, giving of yourself in service, mothering energy aligned with the energy of the Earth. One of the goals of new age lightworkers who have incarnated at this time, is to balance the masculine, aggressive, rational, selfish energy that has dominated the planet for millenia.

Many lightworkers who have predominantly feminine energy have incarnated in male bodies, and are using their position in society to shift the consciousness. Many lightworkers with predominantly masculine energy have incarnated in female bodies to temper their agressive, selfish tendencies. These men in female bodies are using what agression they have to further the cause of women in human structures. The overall process of balancing is necessary to keep humanity from destroying itself as it shifts in focus from ego-centricity to Spirit-centricity.

The advent of the Christ on the Earth began this wave of feminine energy onto the Earth, and the last two thousand years have been a battle of the two opposing principles. This phase is now ending, without any winner, and the balancing of the two is soon to be a reality.

Each of us has the two principles inside of us, and the external struggle has turned into an internal one, as each of us works to balance our own energy in order to become receptive to Spirit. True receptivity and Spiritcentered-ness is only possible when we have conquered the demons of our past, and decide that we need both principles working together in service to Spirit. We must break all our past associations of what it means to be male or female, especially any belief that one or the other is somehow superior. When we release these assumptions, and see each person as a unique combination of both principles, we are on our way to our own personal healing of this issue.

The reason that the feminine is pouring onto the Earth right now is the need for humanity to open and receive Spirit's guidance. This is not possible if the predominant belief system is closed to seeing Spirit as the active force of change that it really is. If a critical mass of humanity does not open to Spirit, then humanity's evolution is at an end. The Creator and his Universal agents cannot allow humanity to move to its next step, the exploration of the cosmos, without a shift in consciousness. This planet was given to humanity in the beginning times to steward, not to destroy through selfish, ego-centered action. If humanity does not correct its attitude, release its arrogance, and acknowledge its source, its time on the Earth will come to a disastrous end. This message has been delivered consistently over the ages, in various forms, without much response. It is very difficult to understand how anyone alive can fail to acknowledge that they are incapable of creating their own life. Yet, somehow, science acts like it can take over the Creator's ability, and do so without Spirit's help. All that science seems to be able to do is invent rediculous means for destroying the life the creator gave them. Any fool can destroy life, but no one but the Creator can create it. Humanity will not continue unless Spirit is given its true understanding and appreciation, and each life is treated as precious, unique and as a gift from the Creator. As long as humanity refuses to open to Spirit, it will flirt with its own destruction. This is just plain common sense.

If humanity opens to the female energy that is arriving here now, then Spirit will begin to guide the affairs of humankind and the future will be the new reality we have all been waiting for. We are seeing a resurgence of the warriors of Spirit on the planet right now. These souls are fed up with the established norms, and they are getting more agressive in removing the obstacles in Spirit's way. Here in America things will soon come to a head, as more and more souls are being denied their Divine inheritance by those who bow to the gods of greed, fear and violence. If these dark souls do not voluntarily shift their consciousness they will be removed, and they will lose their right to advance with the rest of humanity. The choices are very clear right now, and there will not be a continuation of the ways of the past. The past is being dissolved completely, and any who cling to it will be dissolved along with it.

The Earth is leading the way right now, so pay attention to her signals. Align yourself with the Earth's desires, and open to Spiritual guidance. These two things are all you need to do to be in the flow as the transition proceeds on planet Earth. The great cleansing has begun and we are all a big part of it!

Galactic Heritage

There has been a lot of focus lately, in the new age, about "Galactic Heritage". This interest is only natural, since all of us have spent time on other planets, and in other star systems. As well, many other galactic cultures have visited Earth since the beginning times. Many of these visitors interbred with the native Earthlings, and/or experimented genetically on them to produce diiferent versions of the humanoid body form.

Each of us is, therefore, both human, i.e. native to the Earth, and also Galactic/Universal, i.e. genetically speaking and as members of the Universe. There are many, many inhabited worlds in the Universe, but the closest ones to Earth have spent the most time here, and we have spent most of our time on their worlds. These close ones include all the planets in our solar system; the total number of which is 12. The 13th planet was Maldek which was destroyed a long, long time ago. Other cultures that have visited the Earth a lot are the Pleiadians, Sirians, Orions, Lyrans, Antareans, and Arcturans.

The oldest of these cultures, the Arcturans, do not visit the Earth anymore, but they play a strong elder type of role, and all of us have spent time in their system. The Arcturans are immense lightbeings who are very gentle, and who have a large storehouse of information about the galaxy and the Universe. They are the overseers of this part of the galaxy, and all the other cultures consult with them constantly. When galactic travellers return to this sector they check in with the Arcturans, and leave a record with them of their travels. The Arcturans were involved with the earliest age of the Earth, and they guided many of the earliest experiments with physical reality that each of us played such a large role in.

The Antareans are another culture that controls a galactic waystation. They are much more active at this time on the Earth than the Arcturans. Many of the souls that incarnated just after World War 2 on the Earth came through Antares. Antares trains the pioneer/shock troop contingents that come into planetary systems during transition times to shake things up a little. In earlier times on the planet many of the warrior castes were Antares oriented, while those who were connected with the Arcturans were the priests and scribes. All of us have spent many lifetimes experimenting with the Antares and Acturus vibrations.

The planet Maldek was the earliest outpost in our solar system. At that time both Arcturus and Antares were very active and agressive cultures, and they both claimed Maldek as their personal outpost. This difference of opinion over the planet resulted in an escalation of technology to tame Maldek's violent volcanic activity, in order to make it habitable to humanoid forms. This process of "planetforming" has been used all over the galaxy by advanced cultures. Unfortunately, the rivalry between Arcturus and Antares resulted in an accelerated rush to "planetform" Maldek before the planet itself was ready to be tamed. This created a massive explosion that ripped the planet apart, resulting in the debris we now call the asteroid belt. The two competing cultures were both very humbled by this cosmic disaster, and they signed a treaty that from then on they would cooperate to ensure peace and harmony in this region of the galaxy. These elder cultures now maintain outposts on the two furthest planets, planets that will be discovered by human science before the year 2000. This discovery will be the signal for humanity's acceptance into the "Galactic Federation". The headquarters for the Federation locally is on the planet Saturn. Any cultures that desire to observe Earth at this time of transition must get permission from the Saturn Council.

The other planets that figure prominently in our Solar System are Mars and Venus. A very advanced technological culture flourished on Mars after the destruction of Maldek. This culture was founded by a group of Sirians. The Sirians are very mathematically oriented and they like to build pyramids wherever they settle. There are huge pyramid complexes on Mars, some of which still contain records of the civilization that was Martian/Sirian. Mars was a very volcanically active planet, like Maldek, and massive technology was utilized to create an atmosphere on the planet. The machines for this still exist deep below the planet's surface.

The Martian culture lasted a very long time until a cosmic accident occurred that shifted everything. A rogue asteroid entered the Solar System and smashed into the Earth. Hudson Bay in Canada is the crater left by this monster asteroid. This collision altered the orbit of Mars; pushing it away from the Sun and causing a cessation of its volcanism. This vulcanism was used by the Martian/Sirians for the power source of their technology. When it ceased, and the planet began to cool, the Martian/Sirian culture was forced to relocate itself, to Earth.

The other important planet, Venus, was actually further away from the Sun, before the collision, than it is now. It was an outpost for a group of Pleadians at the same time that Mars was in full swing. The Pleaidians are a fun-loving culture. They love sports, games, the arts, and making love; especially making love! Venus was a kind of Pleiadian Club Med back then, and it was absolutely the most beautiful vacation spot in the whole galaxy! Venus was very lush, with lots of water, enormous waterfalls, and spectacular sunsets. Imagine Hawaii, only a million times more incredible, and that was Venus! Unfortunately, when the asteroid hit the Earth, it disturbed Venus' orbit and it had to be abandoned by the Pleadians. They decided to move their Club Med to the Earth.

All of us have a galactic memory encoded in our bodies of all the previous civilizations of the Solar System. We all remember Mars, Venus, Maldek, and all the past we've experienced on the Earth. If you place your consciousness on this you will begin the memory process. If you start to write down your memories you will find that amazing stories will flow from your pen. Now is the time to do this because, after this tranisition on the Earth, all the old stuff will have dissolved away in the new reality. So, if you feel like it, share all your memories with your brothers and sisters.

Now, the other two groups I mentioned were Orion and Lyra. After the Sirians and Pleadians moved to the Earth, they coexisted on opposite sides of the planet. The Sirians built a huge pyramid complex; including the Great Pyramid. They also founded the first technological culture on the Earth, Atlantis. The Pleadians, who called themselves Lemurians on the Earth, continued their fun times; playing games, music, etc. When the two groups did meet they didn't have a lot in common! Meanwhile, the two other groups, Orion and Lyra, were drawn to the Earth and observed the Atlanteans and the Lemurians. The Lyrans were a highly advanced culture whose main preoccupation was music and art of the highest degree. Everything they did turned into an artistic masterpiece. Their songs were so powerful they could use them to rearrange reality! The Lyrans affected both the the Atlanteans and Lemurians, since music is mathematical and is also very good to make love to. The Orion group, on the other hand, were a technological culture who tried to control their whole environment through very precise technological monitoring of everything. Their cities were incredible creations, with infinite levels of precision and codification, all controlled by an advanced technology of the highest order. As you might imagine, the Orions were not drawn to interact with the fun-loving Pleiadians, but they did infiltrate the Atlantean society. They took over their science and began the genetic experimentation on the native forms that everyone was using by now. They also gained control of the Great Crystal which was the central power source of Atlantis. The Orions modified this crystal to be used as a weapon. The Lyrans were aware of the takeover of Atlantis by the Orions, and they warned the Lemurians about it. The Lemurians, of course, were mostly uninterested until their fellows began to disappear to be used by the Orion/Atlanteans for horrible genetic experiments. A small group of Atlanteans were also aware of the infiltration of their society by the Orions, and they tried to warn their fellows, but no one was listening. At this point a group of Lemurians arrived and demanded the return of their missing members. The Orions became afraid for their lives and barricaded themselves in with the Great Crystal, aiming it at the heart of Lemuria. In self-defense, the Lemurians, with help from the Lyrans, set up an harmonic sound wave that traveled around the planet causing earthquakes and volcanic activity. This destabilized the Great Crystal which overamped and blew, sinking all of Atlantis! This upset the Earth so much that she shifted in her orbit, and tipped on her side, causing Lemuria to sink into the ocean. Only a small group of Atlanteans and Lemurians survived, the rest being lost beneath the sea. Thus ended chapter one in the drama of galactic heritage on the Earth!

The World Economy

The economy of the world is in a major tranisition period right now. Since the Industrial Revolution, the main focus of economic activity has been the manufacturing of machinery. The stated goal of this machinery making has always been to reduce the actual physical labor humankind must do. Machines were supposed to free humanity to lead more creative and spontaneous lives. Enormous amounts of capital and resources have been spent to make this dream a reality. The dream, however, has not been universal in its application. The machinery has mostly stayed in the countries that make it, while the resources necessary to create the good life have been stolen from the countries that have them. If those countries objected to the pilfering of their national treasure, they were confronted with violence, and their leaders were bribed or overthrown.

Lately, the developed countries have half-heartedly offered to give the good life to the rest of the world, but mostly greed and violence have been our export specialties. One thing we have been exporting lately has been our system of governing. This has been a function of two factors: First; many of the leaders of developing countries sent their sons and daughters to be educated in the developed world. Of course these leaders stole their countries' wealth to do this, but what the heck! Second; the advent of the Information Age has turned the whole Earth into a giant fishbowl where anyone can get the goods on anything. Even prison nations like China have computers, telephones, televisions, radios and fax machines.

The educated class of the developing world are those born after World War 2, and not coincidentally these souls are part of the first wave of new age lightworkers on the planet. These souls are rapidly forming a critical mass in all the dark areas of the Earth, and beginning the process of change. This change includes education of the masses, popular rebellion, and elections.

As spiritual energy quickens on the Earth, the last areas under the domination of violent, unenlightened souls will shift. The information age is accelerating this process; as the whole world watches a Tiennanmen Square for instance, and focuses their attention on it. This brings the darkness into the light, and once that happens the days of darkness are numbered.

One of the major factors slowing change in the world has been the threat of nuclear annihilation. When a country like China has nuclear weapons they believe themselves to be invulnerable to calls of change from the rest of the world. This nuclear blackmail will soon come to an end. Spirit is in the process of showing certain individuals how to make nuclear warheads harmless through the power of thought. These souls will soon prove their abilities by making it impossible for any country to test their weapons. This will make the whole nuclear arsenal useless, and the threat of planetary destruction will never occur again.

The 1992 U.S. election will be a referendum of sorts for world consciousness. As we said, the world economy is shifting and the industrial age is winding down. Machinery will not be the agent of freedom for the common human. Information will be the first step towards the new reality. Information leads to enlightened choices, and everyone will be exposed to a bonanza of choices as we near the 1992 election. A huge number of Americans are homeless and jobless due to the immense greed of a few ugly souls. 1992 will bring this dark tale into the open and everyone will have a choice. The greedy can choose to distribute their wealth back to those they stole it from, or they will find it taken back by the agents of Spirit. Each individual must choose to take back their power, and hold others responsible for thelr actions. America has stolen the world's resources to make Americans comfortable. This has caused resentment around the globe, and the world is clamoring for a return of those resources in some form. Americans, and the rest of the developed world, are going to have to change to a simpler, more honest lifestyle.

The power of Spirit will begin to expose the deeds of those who have stolen from their brothers and sisters. These souls will be held accountable by those they have stolen from, and they will be forced to make a choice. The control freaks, who envision a one world government that will line their pockets, are in for a rude awakening! Consciousness on the Earth has reached a critical juncture and the meek will inherit what the greedy have stolen.

In the end, the world economy is the sum of each individual's desire to be free, to be peaceful, and to manifest the personal dream they chose this lifetime. The Earth and Spirit are lending their energies to this quest, and the new reality is being created every moment we are alive. As the world is informed, and makes choices, the old ways of fear, greed, and violence shall dissolve into the peace of a new age. As you attune to the inner guidance, all the shifts in the world make perfect sense, and you can begin to see the new reality wherever you look. The grace of Spirit is in the world now, and now is the time to create with Spirit the new dream; the same dream we all dreamed together so long ago!

Dreams

Dreams are extremely important right now. During this transition humankind is moving from a highly physical mode of being into a more Spirit-based existence. As we move into the lull period between the ways, we enter the Great Void, or silence, that is the Divine. When we are in this void, we exist on all levels of reality simultaneously, without our usual ability to filter what we want to experience. This puts enormous pressure on our bodies and nervous systems, which become overloaded with input and tend to shut down. This is the reason that all spiritual systems teach some form of meditation as a beginning exercise. Meditation allows a controlled shutdown of the body so that we can relax and open all our circuits to receive information. As we transit the Great Void any form of meditation will be very helpful. Many of us will find that we are meditating and sleeping a great deal these days. This will become even more necessary as we transit the Great Void. Sleep is even more important than meditation for complete body relaxation. When we sleep, we dream, and this is how Spirit can connect our higherself to our lower-self. There are many messages that our higher-self needs to give to our lower-self. Our conscious mind tends to block out these messages, even during meditation. During sleep, as we dream, these messages can be delivered without being blocked. The more we have strong ego-awareness while we are awake, the more we will find ourselves sleeping as the transition proceeds. Many of our dreams may take on nightmarish, doomsday qualities as the higher-self urges the lower-self to release all its fears, and as the body releases pent-up memories.

Many of the immune disorder diseases that we are seeing on the planet right now relate directly to this transit of the void. Peoples' bodies are becoming over-inputted, yet they still refuse to slow down. This puts too much of a strain on their physical systems, and their bodies collapse. The so-called "yuppie disease" is a good example of this. When the input people receive is contradictory to their personal "ego-beliefsystem", and they try to block out the information coming from Spirit, this can sometimes cause a complete shutdown, i.e. a coma or a stroke. Everyone must open to Spirit's messages at this time, or leave their body. Therefore, we must all trust in the Divine, release our attatchments to the world, meditate and sleep a lot, and allow our dreams to inform us of Spirit's intentions.

In 1992 we will begin to see a lot of external shifts, signalling our transit of the void. We can use these as signposts for our own internal transition; to see where we are on the curve. If you find that you have transitted early, and you have a lot of extra energy, then turn and help your brothers and sisters to transit. This is all there really is to do right now, and all resistance and any claims to the contrary will only cause a lot of personal pain. Relax, release, meditate, sleep, dream, and connect with Spirit. If you do this fully, your life will be in flow with the cosmos, and you will never be the same again.

Joy

The message of Joy is permeating everything right now. This is only natural, because we are returning to our original state, which was Joy. In the beginning times we only had one state of being, and that was Joy. It was only after we became trapped in physical form that we began to experience all the emotions we do now. We identified with our bodies, which became so real to us that we believed that we couldn't leave them. We also identified with our emotions and became trapped by them as well. Slowly, over eons of time, we have been learning to dis-identify with our bodies. On a higher level this is why there has been so much violence on our planet. Over time, as we were killed, left our bodies, and returned, we learned that bodies weren't permanent, but that we were. It has taken an enormous amount of time for everyone to get this one because physical existence seems so real.

Now we are all working on releasing our emotions. As we do this fully, the only thing that we will feel inside our being is Joy. We are all lightbeings of infinite Joy!

As we become dis-identified with our bodies and emotions, we are left with our thoughts. Thought is the most ethereal of the illusion realities. It is also the easiest for us to change because it is the most fluid. Thought creates all the other illusion realities. In the truest sense, we are our thoughts! As you change your mind you change the world. As we watch our thoughts pass into, and out of, existence, in a moment of time, we can understand how impermanent thoughts really are. It is only when our thoughts become fixated, that we become stuck in time, and we lose our true self in the illusion. Spiritual teachings teach us to dis-identify with our thoughts if we want to become free. If you totally dis-identify with your thoughts, you will lose all association with any beliefs, expectations, and opinions you may hold about the world or yourself. Suddenly, you will find that all of those things were just arbitrary judgements. These judgements had become fixated in your thought stream causing a blockage of the flow that your thought was meant to have. If you unblock the stream, then all the thoughts of God will pass through your mind.

You will become aware of all there is to know in the Universe! You will become enlightened! Anything you desire to know will appear in your mind without any effort on your part at all. You must simply release any attatchment to your body, your emotions, and your thoughts.

As you release these things they don't go away; they actually become more accessible to you for your creative use. They become like the palette of an artist; always available for a beautiful painting. No true artist would ever become so fixated on his palette that he would believe that he was to use only one of his colors. He would want to use the full range of all the colors, to mix and match at will, and create a rich variety of hues to paint his masterpiece. In the same way, we must dis-associate ourselves from what is not us, so we are left with what we are; co-creators with the Divine impulse. We can still use the magnificent palette of body, emotion, and thought to create our masterpieces of life. When we create as lightbeings of pure Joy, our creations are fully aligned with the flow of the cosmos, and they express the full range of the Divine.

This is the future of humanity. We are all participating in the transition shift to Joyful, Spirit-based, co-creating. As we begin this shift, as the Joy of Spirit permeates our being, all our fixations and associations will come up for us to review. We will find ourselves playing many different roles; sometimes simultaneously! We will have outbursts of emotion. We will become aware of all our sticky thoughts. We will find our beliefs and opinions challenged. We will feel our bodies changing. We will become very confused about who we really are. All of this will lead us to the brink of the Great Void, where we will pause and glance back at all we thought, felt, and believed we were. Then we will turn and leap into the void, to become lightbeings of pure Joy, creating from the palette of illusion, without attatchment, and just for the fun of it! We will soar and dive with the ebb tide of the cosmic flow, attuned to the Divine impulse, and glowing brightly on into the future.

Desire

Desire is the main motivating factor on the Earth right now. Desire functions in two ways: One; it keeps humanity on the move, always seeking something more, always trying out the latest thing. In this way it can help humanity to grow, progress, and evolve. Two; desire takes us out of our moment, away from the Divine union of the present, and into a future that always seems to declare itself bigger, better, and more special than the present. In this way desire takes us away from the path of just being with God, and sends us into the wilderness of ego-action and ego-fulfillment.

This is the cosmic parpadox: without desire for life, for experience, we would never have moved away from the presence of the Divine, and out to explore the potential of the Universe. However, once out here, we have become enmeshed in the illusion of desire, and we have forgotten how to just be and appreciate all that we are and all that surrounds us. We have reached the precipice of self-awareness, only to forget our roots. We have begun to believe that we are self-sufficient, that we do not need our Creator. This desire to be all-powerful has created the dilemna of the times; immanent self-destruction! It is as if we are taunting God, saying: " save us from ourselves, if you can!". This is totally nuts! We must learn to shift this, to embrace the paradox of creation, to trust in ourselves and Spirit, to move into a true holy relationship with the Universe, and to love the Earth. There is nothing to prove through self-destructing, and everything to gain by using our desire to become closer to God. The key is never to deny what we have been given, in this case desire, but to utilize it in a sacred manner for the benefit of ourselves and creation.

Because we have free will, we can co-create an infinite array of realities. So why would we choose the path of fear, greed, violence, and self-destruction? Is our destiny to love and desire death above all else? Are we to give up the beauty that is all around us, and inside us, for the pathway of illusive self-aggrandizement and delusion? I think not! A small group, of small minds, has been let loose on the planet so that we may all become aware of the consequences of our actions. Each day that we are alive, we become more aware of this small group of fanatics that desire nothing but death. Well I say: let us grant them their wish! Let us declare them "persona non grata" in the world of love and compassion that we are co-creating with Spirit! Let us declare, that as admission to Heaven on Earth, they must release their desire for death and embrace a desire for life. They must lay down their weapons and self-importance. They must decide that they didn't create themselves. They must accept that they are not the final arbiters of humankind's destiny! They must acknowledge that science is an abberation, that true knowledge comes from union with the Divine. They must give up all their petty wars and become peaceful. Let them desire all this and they will be welcome in the world that we are co-creating. If not, then we will release them to their own destruction. Why should we delay our own dreams, our own destiny, for a stupid bunch of dark fanatics who don't even know how foolish they look to the rest of the Universe? No!!! The time has come to re-create the Heaven we left so long ago. Our true destiny awaits us, and nothing can stop us from rejoining the creator. Nothing!!! We have made up our minds, and we have freed ourselves from the delusional creations of madmen. We are free to begin the new reality on the Earth. We are in the Creator's hands, and we have released the ego-reality and embraced the cosmic paradox. We are our own future. We are beyond the grasp of illusion. We have embodied the truth on Earth, and our time is now!!!

Destiny

What exactly is "Destiny"? It is, quite simply, the path back to God that we each chose when we came to Earth. It is our personal roadmap, that leads us through each of the experiences that will prepare us for our reunion with the Divine. Often, we include in our destiny path chance encounters with those souls we have met on our previous visits here. These meetings are like signposts on our path that remind us where we've been and where we're going. Our destiny road is usually quite wide to accomodate a broad range of experience, but sometimes we can choose a narrow road that gives us a fast track back to God. Often, all of our experiences on the path seem to have a common thread running through them, a certain theme we have chosen this time around.

After we have chosen our destiny, in the higher realms, we make agreements with those souls who will be our parents on the Earth. We often choose our parents on the basis of previous soul- connections in past lives, and on their affinity towards the soul path we have chosen. Once we come to the Earth, our destiny is shrouded from us, and we begin the magical journey of rediscovering the destiny we chose, reconnecting with those souls we chose to meet on the way, and actualizing our true destiny path on the Earth.

As we journey through life, we often find that certain elements of our journey seem to be beyond our personal control. It seems that some things just happen to us without our personal will activating them. These chance experiences are the crossroads, the signposts that we placed on our path to aid us in our journey. These can take many forms, but always they will stand out in our memory, and they will usually signal a lifeshift of some sort. Even if our life tends to be very ordinary, these destiny nodepoints tend to jump out at us, causing us to sort of wake up and take notice. Destiny nodes often can take on a "life or death" kind of scenario, depending on our particular path and how aligned we are with it. Astrologers talk about the "Saturn Return" as an example of a destiny node that affects each of us. Saturn Return tends to cause us to stop our headlong rush through life long enough to review what we've done, who we've been, and what we'd like to do/be in the future. In extreme cases, if our external reality has affected us greatly, we find that we are off our destiny path, and a strong node point experience may be necessary to place us back on our path. Often, in these cases, our soul guides intervene. A soul guide is a soul that is disembodied and has an affinity for a particular soul on the Earth. These guides stay in contact with their Earth souls, and act to help them to actualize their destiny. Depending on our particular destiny, we may have a number of soul guides who take on particular roles as we need them.

At certain points on our path it is important that we make a choice. These are the times when we need to actualize a certain element of our destiny. At these times we will find that anything we try to do that is not part of this particular destiny activation will not manifest. This can be very frustrating if we are not conscious at all of our destiny. At these times our guides will place obstacles in our path to prevent us from deviating from our chosen destiny. We can resist as much as we want, but we are only resisting the destiny we ourselves chose before we came to Earth.

There is also what is known as soul-group destiny. The time period on the Earth we choose to incarnate into gives us a clue as to our soulgroup path. As the Earth begins to transition, from physical, egocentered reality to Spirit-centered reality, many of us will begin to activate our chosen group destiny. Each soul-group has picked a certain activity that will help the Earth in this important time. Much of what we have chosen to do relates to what we have done in the past as a group-mind. As we find ourselves drawn to certain types of people, or to certain areas of the Earth, this past soul-activity will come into our consciousness, and it will signal a strong remembrance of what we have chosen to activate this time. Starting right after World War 2, whole waves of us began to incarnate together to begin the process of transition. The first wave were the shock troops of Spirit. These souls chose to break things wide open, questioning everything that had been happening for many millenia on the Earth. This group was very psychically attuned and really began to activate their destiny in the mid-1 960's. They were the bridge to the next wave,which is not quite as active on the physical but very active on the subtle realms. The first wave were the warriors of light, who did not wish to compromise their integrity at all, and felt it necessary to fight against the status quo whenever possible. The second wave stayed more hidden, and watched the reactions against the first wave by the established powers on the Earth. Now, the second wave has had time to integrate all they have seen, and experienced, and they have spent time with the first wave to appreciate their point of view. The second wave can now begin to use their knowledge of subtle energy to affect consciousness on the planet. This is the second wave's destiny path; to activate the blueprint of the new reality that is in the ethereal plane, and begin to bring that blueprint down to the Earth. The first wave opened the gates by removing obstacles to the new energy. Now, the second wave can bring the energy through the gates and into physical manifestation.

Each of us, therefore, has a part to play in the unfolding of Spirit's plan on the Earth. As we begin to activate our destiny, we will begin to meet in larger and larger groups; first in the astral realms, through meditation, and then, more and more, in the physical. As we begin to remember the way to translate into and out of the physical, this distinction will not be as obvious. In the next few years, however, we will be shown the way to gather as a soul-group, and through this gathering we will activate the blueprint on the Earth. As you match your personal destiny with your soul-group destiny, Spirit will come to you and show you what must be done and where to do it. As you share your personal dream with others you will begin to see how all of our dreams interweave, and you will get strong glimpses of the great pattern we are creating with Spirit. As you get these glimpses, share them with as many of your soul-group as you can to activate their remembrance, their personal destiny, and the cosmic blueprint. We are all activators at this crucial time, co-creating with Spirit the new reality for our planet and the Universe itself.

The Function
of the
Sun

The Sun serves many different purposes for us in our reality. The Sun is the guardian of the external reality. It provides support for our bodies and for all lifeforms on earth. It also informs the external reality, through its rays, acting as a conduit for spiritual information from the Central Sun of our galaxy. The sun is also a larger version of the divine light that each of us contains within us. In this way the sun can be seen as a role model for us. Each of us is a small sun/star constantly shining our light on all we contact. The Sun has its own consciousness and its own evolution. It caretakes all of the planets in the solar system, that is its service. It uses its light to advise all of the planets, and the lifeforms on them, and to keep their various outer forms functioning. The sun is also the source of much higher knowledge and inspiration. It helps to step down Spirit's message into a medium that we, as humans, can absorb and utilize. Early civilizations on earth were more conscious of this mechanism, and made the mistake of worshipping the sun. As a created being, the Sun is not a god, but it does protect, enliven, and inspire us while we inhabit the earth.

The elementals use the sun's information stream to maintain all of the lifeforms of the earth. Because of humankind's altering of the atmosphere, through pollution, it is difficult for the elementals to get a clear stream of information in many areas of the earth. Certain magnetic waves generated by machinery are also detrimental to this process. It is impossible for our bodies to exist, in their current form, for very long without the Sun. Human souls who live in cities, and do not receive the fullness of the Sun's information, often become diseased after a while. The parts of their bodies that are not informed by the Sun, will lose their lifeforce, atrophy, and die.

As we learn to source spiritual energy directly from the source of all things, our bodies will change, and we will not need the Sun as an intermediary any more. This will free the Sun to move on in its own evolutionary path. A long time ago, the earth was not tipped on its axis, and its pole pointed at the Central Sun. Earth, and its inhabitants, received direct spiritual guidance at this time. The Sun's service at this time was on the level of physical light only. When Atlantis destroyed itself, and the Earth shifted her axis, it became difficult to receive direct guidance, and the Sun took on the mantle of spiritual intermediary for us all. Now we are moving back into allignment with the true source, through conscious choice, in partnership with the Earth. As the Earth shifts consciousness, and we join her, her axis will tilt once again, and we will become fully alligned once again with the Central Sun. Our Sun is supporting us with this shift, and it has much to share with us as we begin to shift. If you make a mind connection with the Sun, ask for guidance and insight for yourself and the planet. You can ask the elementals to help you with this. The stronger your conscious connection with the Sun, the easier your shift will be, and the more information you will be able to share with the rest of us. Remember, we are all part of the Milky Way galaxy as well; that is our greater soul group. As we shift our consciousness, it affects the whole galactic matrix. Our new light shoots back down the spiral to the center of the galaxy, which in return is informed and shifts, sending new light our way. This is the pattern of evolution in our galaxy. It is always a two way flow, never ending its movement towards greater consciousness for all of us, the sparks of god.

The White Brotherhood

The White Brotherhood has been active on the Earth for eons of time. It is composed of evolved souls who have made the shift to spirit-centered living, and desire to help others do the same. One of the functions of the Brotherhood has been to keep records of all that has occurred on the Earth, and to safeguard those records from harm during transitional times. These records are stored in many locations around the world, beneath the ground, and inside mountains. The most famous record room is beneath the great Sphinx in Egypt. Some parts of this room will be discovered before the year 2000, to aid humanity in remembering its past so that it may transit to the future. Many of us now incarnated on Earth have spent time as active members of the Brotherhood, safeguarding the records and adding to them as events unfold.

Another function of the White Brotherhood has been to keep the true knowledge during periods of darkness on Earth. As forces of fear and ignorance seek to take over control of the Earth, the Brotherhood actively counters this by informing humanity of its past, and passing on the true understanding to those who can listen. After past great cataclysms on the Earth, the White Brotherhood patiently educated the survivors so that the evolution of humanity would not slip backwards. The White Brotherhood is actually a universal organization, whose members are active across the Universe, helping planetary cultures to survive and evolve.

Much of what the Brotherhood does is hidden from the mass of humanity. This is on purpose, because each individual must walk his own path at his own pace. The Brotherhood watches, guides, and protects those who are actively seeking the light, but it does not seek to influence those who are unconscious servants of fear and ignorance. The Brotherhood knows that all things happen at the right time for each of us, and they are not impatient.

In the last century or so, the Brotherhood has sought those who are open enough, and they have shared their wisdom with these souls, who have then shared what they learned with others. This channelling of the members of the Brotherhood allowed them to stay hidden, while at the same time get the message out. Occasionally they have decided to appear to certain individuals to impress them more fully with the importance of the message. Joseph Smith, who founded the Mormon faith, is a good example of this. The records he was given access to were extremely important for his time period, and so the the Brotherhood sent a messenger to him.

Many, many people have had encounters with brothers, in the physical, and some have been taken to record rooms to bear witness to others of the truth of their existence. All of this has been to prepare the denser souls for what is beginning to occur now. As the Earth begins to transit from the physical, the Brotherhood's story and the whole record of the Earth until now, will become common knowledge. Many of the record rooms will be opened up, and the truth will be revealed. Of course each of us will see and hear only what we are open to, for this is natural spiritual law. But the forces of ignorance and fear will not be able to stop the truth from being available to anyone who desires to know it. This will aid each soul in making a clear choice; to either stay in ego-centered reality, or move into allignment with Spirit.

As the transition moves along, many of us will reconnect not just with our past lives, as part of the White Brotherhood, but with current members of the Brotherhood. Some of us may choose to translate out of the physical, to be with them during the transition. Others of us will be actively engaged in physical reality to help our brothers and sisters align with Spirit. Many of us will continue to bring out the message of truth in whatever form we can.

Ask for attunement to the White Brotherhood at this time, if you feel this is part of your dharma, and open to the possibility of channelling the records into a book or other form. This is important work at this stage of the transition, and it will prepare you for whatever you have chosen to do as the Earth-shift intensifies in the next few years.

We are all brothers and sisters of the White Brotherhood, we have all been nurtured by our Earthmother, and we all await the great shift of consciousness that is occurring, at this very moment, on our planet Earth.

The Function of Personality

Another term for the ego is personality. Each of us has a part of ourselves that we show to the world, and a part that we keep hidden. The external mask that we present is a conglomeration of all we have accumulated around ourselves in our eons of time travelling the universe.

One function of the personality is to allow us to fit in with the planet and society we have incarnated in. This allows us to integrate ourselves into our environment, to feel that we somehow belong in our external reality, so that we do not feel alien. Many of us however, do not feel assimilated into the Earth culture, no matter how hard we try. Often this can be a function of where we were before we came to Earth. Many of us spend much of our time travelling in our light bodies around the universe, and interacting with non-physical cultures. We often only spend time in the physical realms when our services are needed during transitional times, such as the time we are experiencing here right now.

When we come to Earth, for instance, we veil who we really are by layering ourselves with personality, so that we do not cause fear in those who are attatched to the physical reality. We have become experts at forgetting ourselves, while we grow up in the world, and we become part of the planetary matrix. Depending on our destiny path, we may not begin to shed this external cover until just before we are ready to actualize our unique purpose on the Earth.

The process of uncovering ourselves has been likened to unpeeling an onion, layer by layer, but this does not have to be so. It all depends on the individual, and how enmeshed in the world he/she has become. If we have remained conscious of our true self, throughout our incarnation, we may simply shrug off our personality covering, at the appropriate moment, and fulfill our destiny.

Often we may opt to use our personality as a filter mechanism, shining our true self through the ego to manifest a particular action, or influence a certain individual or group, without drawing attention to ourselves.

For many souls who choose to "walk-in" to the planet, occupying a body they did not grow up in, the process first involves assimilating their soul energy with the personality they have beamed into. This can be a difficult process if the soul that left the planet had become too identified with the external manifestation. Often energy leaks can occur that will bring strong reactions from those souls who are still unconscious. Again, if assimilation occurs, the "walk-in" can use the layers of personality as a filter, and project their truth through it to enact transformation of the highest order on the planet. Presently there are millions of souls doing just this to help heal the planetary imbalance on Earth.

For those of us who have incarnated, and veiled ourselves, now is our time to release all the layers of the ego we do not need, and allow Spirit to flow through what personality remains. In this way we will be guided to the places, and events, that we have chosen that fit our personal identity matrix needed to actualize our soul path for this lifetime.

All the difficulties that arise on the Earth are due to personality conflicts. Often this is due to a soul taking on layers that do not fit their true pattern. Each of us needs to listen deeply to our inner guidance of what we truly need, and release what is not us. If this seems to bother those close to us, that is o.k. See the true self inside the layers of those who are affected, and ask for guidance to help them release the veils that are not helping them in their task. This is delicate work, but essential at this time if Spirit is to manifest to the greatest degree possible. A clue to aid you in this is to listen to what an individual says, realizing what is reaction and what is true understanding. Then realize that they are speaking to themselves, that they really desire to release that reaction layer because it is not helping them. If you can show them they are in reaction, not seeing in a true way, they can begin the process of releasing, allowing them to manifest more of who they really are.

Over the next few years we will all release our unneeded layers of personality, and align ourselves with Spirit to manifest Heaven on Earth. This is why we are here. So listen closely to yourself, and others, and aid your brothers and sisters to hone their ego-self to the essence of their destiny path. Then we will all be ready to act on what we know is our Divine destiny this time around.

The Hollow Earth

Many New-Agers are interested in the Hollow Earth Theory, but they are not sure what to make of the idea. The truth is that the Earth itself is not hollow, but that many of us have genetic memory of living inside the Earth a long time ago. Much of Atlantis was built underground, with enormous cavernous chambers, and an intricate system of tunnels linking them with eachother and the upper world. Many of the disastrous scientific experiments occurred deep beneath the Earth, where there wasn't much hope for escape for the Lemurians that were held captive. Eventually the tunnel network reached into Lemuria itself, and these were used by the scientists to escape detection as they kidnapped Lemurians. Eventually the Lemurians discovered this network, and what had happened to their fellow Lemurians there, and this led to the conflict that destroyed both cultures.

After the fall of Atlantis, as the Earth began the chaos that would shift her axis, a number of Lemurians escaped into the tunnel network, and they lived in there for quite a long time. When the Earth shifted, many of the tunnels and caverns were broken, and many of the different groups living beneath the Earth had to travel great distances to find their way to the surface. When they emerged, the world had changed, and each group had to fend for themselves, creating unique cultures and mythologies based on what they remembered of Atlantis, Lemuria, and their time beneath the Earth.

As we said, in a previous section, some of the Atlanteans escaped and tried to recreate Atlantis after the shift. These scientists founded what would become the Egyptian civilization a long time after the shift. They were never quite successful in recreating Atlantis, and the pure Atlantean culture died out because their gene pool was too small. Many of their genetic experiments, which they had brought out of Atlantis, were remembered later in Egyptian and Greek mythology.

The Lemurians founded the civilizations of pre-Indian, pre-Tibetan, pre-Incan, pre-Mayan, pre-Aboriginal, and others that are lost to us now. All of these were destroyed in the great deluge that occurred during the last Earth shift before the present. None of these cultures reached the technological mastery of Atlantis, or the psychic attunement of Lemuria. When the deluge came, the Lemurian influenced cultures once again escaped into the tunnels and survived. When they emerged. they founded the cultures we now consider as native or ethnic. Each of these has kept a record of their journeys into the Earth during times of cataclysm, and they enact ceremonies and rituals to keep these remembrances alive. Many of their mythologies speak of a strange brother or sister who warned them of impending dangers, or who they met while they were underground. These were members of the White Brotherhood, whose destiny is not only to keep records of the Earth but to also make sure that a remnant of humanity survives through any Earth calamity. The brotherhood keeps the record rooms veiled by a dimensional shift, so only those of Spirit can enter, but they watch over humanity, and will act to help if help is needed. Some members of the White Brotherhood, that live in vast underground cities, have chosen to come to the surface at this time to share their knowledge with humanity. It is possible, if one is pure of intention, to enter the tunnel network and connect directly with the Brotherhood. If you desire to do so, ask for contact with a Brotherhood member on the surface, open to Spirit-centered living, and move into a city of light away from the urban chaos and ego-reality. In the next few years some of us will make the journey back into time, beneath the surface of the Earth, to connect with our brothers and sisters of the hollow Earth.

Abundance

We are all truly abundant beings. Abundance happens when we dance with the "Abun", the breath of God. When we are one with the breath, we are in perfect harmony with the Divine Inspiration, and we are in flow with Spirit's plan in a state of grace. Abundance is our natural state because we are all children of God, and we are all created from God's breath and song. The only thing that can stop us from being abundant, is ourselves. If we choose not to dance with Divine Inspiration, and decide instead to follow our own plan for ourselves, we find ourselves dancing with the ego-reality and hitting walls wherever we go. Because we are free-will beings, we can choose to be abundant or not. The Divine wants us to be inspired and blessed, but it will not be forced upon us. If we decide to experience pain, effort, struggle, and lack, Spirit will not interfere. Spirit has infinite patience, and will always be waiting when we are ready to return to our natural state.

The external world that we are inhabiting at this time is a mixture of each of these elements. The Earth has allowed us to be here to experience on all levels what ego-reality is like. The Earth itself is an abundant being, and we can contact her when we wish to remember our true selves. What humanity has created is an ego-reality, disconnected from the Divine, and we can experience it as much as we desire. Through experiencing the two different ways of being, we can feel the difference, and make a personal choice of how we wish to live.

Many, many souls are now deciding to return to abundance at this time. Each of them have spent eons of time experiencing ego-reality, and they are ready to release it fully to embrace the dance of the Divine. As this happens, our world will change to become more and more an expression of abundance. It will become much easier to feel the grace of God. In a very short period of time our world will be fully abundant, as each of us returns to the original state of being and flows with Divine Inspiration. The ego-world will seem to have simply vanished, and we will not even remember the strange journey we took away from the Divine.

Love between
Men and Women

Everything in this external reality is of a dual nature: male/female, dark/light, positive/negative, etc.. When we are in the astral, waiting to incarnate, each of us pictures what we'd like to accomplish in our incarnation, and we tend to categorize these accomplishments according to whether they are personal, or global, in scope. At the core of all of our dreams is the desire to manifest Divine Love on the Earth. In the beginning times we did not take on the duality in our forms, we simply observed it in our environment, but some of us desired to experience what we saw more intimately. As we began to experiment with this embodying of the duality, our forms took on the appearance that corresponded to our personal experience. After eons of time, our forms have become more and more distinct, as our differences became solidified around one pole or the other. What is important to remember here is that all of this is our choice, it is in our consciousness. We can decide to change who we are, at all levels, any time we want. As we took on distinct forms, we assigned the roles that each form would take, and this role playing changed according to our beliefs of where we came from. Many early cultures were obsessed with the wonder of the birth process, and thus they formed matriarchal societies to worship the feminine, creative form/role. Later societies became equally obsessed with the powers of the rational mind, and set up patriarchal societies, worshiping the ability to use the mind to know the world, and to create new things. These latter societies denigrated women and God, believing that we were just animals with powerful minds, obviously forgetting where those minds came from. Some of these scientists actually believe that some day soon they will create life without God. This is of course totally nuts, but it illustrates the extent that we have gone to try and explore the polarities of duality.

Today we find ourselves at the end of an experiment with the rational pole, one that has led us to the edge of self-destruction. We are caught in a cosmic catch-22 here, as some desire to experience absolute polarization, and others feel that to do that would be to risk extinction as a culture. At this point it appears that the collective consciousness, at least unconsciously, has chosen the path of union rather than dissolution. Those souls who still desire the absolute experience will most likely have to incarnate on another planet to experience it.

Our journey towards reunion, on a planetary scale, brings us back to our topic: the love between men and women. Each of us, at a core level, has as our incarnative purpose the desire to manifest Divine Love on the Earth. Since each of us is Divine Love embodied, on the truest level, this means we must each express our true selves on the Earth. Because we are in forms that have taken on one or the other pole of duality, to express who we really are we must balance the polarized elements within us. Some spiritual disciplines ask us to do this on our own, using various methods that all ask us to refrain from encounters with the opposite polarity. This, on a common sense level, makes no sense. How can we incorporate both poles in our being if we are constantly pushing one pole away from us? No! The only way to balance and express our true self, is to fully embrace all the aspects of duality, and create the cosmic fusion that will make us whole. This is the whole reason for our incarnating at this level of reality; to be whole, and through our wholeness bring our Divine nature fully to Earth. One way to create this is to express your love for the opposite polarity fully! As you do this the poles in your being will respond, open up, and express themselves, and you will become who you really are. The great tantric teachings of India are all expressing this principle. Embrace all that you see, and love it fully, and you will be healed, whole, and enlightened. You will become you!

Because all that we experience here is part of the duality, we can embrace it all, and through our embrace we can know it all and become it all. This is the true nature of enlightenment; self awareness through the fusion of opposites, and the complete love of all things. If you love it all, you become it all, and you become yourself, because you contain it all. If you start by loving your cosmic polarity mate, and you fuse energies, you will begin the process whose only outcome can be the complete manifestation of your Divine nature, which is all there truly is.

The Anti-Christ

On the highest level, the emergence of the Anti-Christ is simply the manifestation of ego-centered reality throughout the world. All that is not universally Spirit-centered, unconditionally loving, and totally conscious, can be considered a manifestation of the Anti-Christ on the Earth. As we move into this period of transition, from ego to Spirit, the polarity between the two will become more and more obvious, and our choices to act from one or the other will become more distinct. Each of us will have to turn to our inner guidance, constantly, in order to distinguish between the false and true realities. We will not be able to rely on external advice or external appearance to make the true choice. Our only reliance must be on Spirit's voice coming through our inner knowingness. When we rely on externalized information for our choices, we open ourselves up to the negative, ego-oriented, fear-based manifestations of the Anti-Christ. If we rely on seductive, false information, we join our individual karma with the collective karma of the Apocalypse. We become ensnared with all those souls who choose to be destroyed, rather than aligning ourselves with Spirit and the Divine. As with everything we do, the choice is always ours. If you rely on external authority for your salvation, you will not save yourself! You must turn to the inner light of Spirit, and when you you do all will become clear and you will be moved away from the collective karma that brings destruction, chaos, fear, and death.

In the next few years, as the polarity between ego and Spirit become ever more clear, you will be continually asked to make a commitment to one or the other. The sooner you commit to Spirit, the sooner you will be transported away from the destructive ego-reality and placed with those who understand the truth. Your commitment to Spirit is the signal that will open up the infinite truth of the Divine plan to your awareness. Without this commitment you will never find this understanding, even if you seek it for the rest of eternity. With your commitment to Spirit, your heart will open, and your life will be a continual series of revelations and inspirations. Without a spiritual commitment you will constantly be exposed to the violent death-throes of the ego-based world, and you will perish in the prophetic end of the world scenario created by humankind's insistence on the denial of Spirit. No one can claim ignorance of these facts because Spirit is in touch with each of us continuously, whether we are listening or not!

From 1992-1996 we will be confronted, on an accelerating exponential basis, with an endless array of true and false choices. These are designed to force us to rely on our intuition, our inner awareness, and our connection to the Divine. As with anything practice makes perfect, so now is the time to cultivate your inner guidance and become completely grounded and centered in this connection. After 1996, the Anti-Christ will have complete control over the externalized, ego-based world, and the ultimate manifestation of this false reality will rise into the collective awareness, in human form, sometime in late 1996 or early 1997. The years from then until the year 2000 will be a literal Hell on Earth for those still unwilling to open to Spirit, and it will become increasingly difficult for the personal shift to be made the longer the Anti-Christ is in power. So remember, now is the time to fully commit and align with Spirit, to practice relying on your inner awareness, and to open your heart to the Divine plan so you may be placed in your right place; away from the crumbling, dissolving ego-world we see all around us. As with all things, we must believe in something for it to be real. As long as we believe in a false reality, it will be real for us. Once we become fully aware of the truth, nothing else is real, and we are literally unaffected by anything that is false. This is your key to this time. Align with the truth and Spirit, and all else will follow in effortless grace, beauty and understanding.

May Peace Prevail On the
Earth, Now And Forevermore!

GREETINGS!

****

EL MORYA IS AN ASCENDED MASTER WHO LIVES UNDER THE EARTH IN THE CITY OF SHAMBALLA. HE IS VERY INTERESTED IN HELPING HUMANITY THROUGH THIS TIME OF TRANSITION, AND HE ENJOYS SHARING STORIES AND WISDOM WITH ANYONE WHO HAS THE TIME TO LISTEN. TO REACH HIM JUST DIAL UP YOUR INNER-EAR PHONE AND ASK FOR EL MORYA. * HE'LL GET IN TOUCH! *

****

SHEM EMMANUEL IS AN ORDINARY HUMAN, WHO LIVES ON THE SURFACE OF THE EARTH, AND TRIES TO PUT DOWN HIS MUDDLED PERCEPTIONS OF REALITY AS THIS TIME OF TRANSITION FLIES BY. SO FAR SHEM HAS PUT OUT A MUSIC TAPE CALLED "MASSAGE MEDITATION", AND NOW THIS BOOK. HE CAN BE REACHED AT THE ADDRESS IN THE FRONT COVER OF THIS BOOK.